SQL

The Ultimate Beginner's Step-by-Step Guide to Learn SQL Programming with Hands-On Projects

Written By

Brandon Cooper

Brandon Cooper

derived from various sources. Please consult a licensed professional before attempting any techniques outlined in this book.

By reading this document, the reader agrees that under no circumstances is the author responsible for any losses, direct or indirect, that are incurred as a result of the use of information contained within this document, including, but not limited to, errors, omissions, or inaccuracies.

Brandon Cooper

Contents

Introduction

The SQL database contains many ins and outs that process queries in reference to the data fed to it. If that sounds like a mouthful, there is no need to worry. This book is designed to walk you through how to set up your own database using the SQL language and to create a foundation for your company.

This book is designed with your needs in mind. Once you begin your own SQL system, you can use this book as both a step-by-step guide and a reference for further questions. The examples and sample queries and tables listed in the table are included to make your transition to the SQL system as quick and painless as possible.

SQL is unlike other programming languages, as it was initially designed to only maintain tables within the database and access them over time. However, as SQL has improved over the several decades of its existence, it has evolved to create processes and store them for future use. SQL databases today format information through placing data in tables. This data is accessed through *queries*, the language used to communicate with a database through a relational database management system.

Who Is This For?

Brandon Cooper

If you are new to programming and SQL, this beginner's guide is designed to take you through how to complete simple and complex tasks with tables and sample queries included to make practicing easier. The book is designed to take the guesswork out of creating your own database and make setting up a business even easier.

If you are reading this book to learn more about the programming world, hats off to you. This book is designed to make the transition from knowing nothing about programming to giving you an in-depth resource into its system.

If you are an advanced learner with a solid base in the SQL programming, this book contains advanced elements throughout its pages to benefit you on your continued quest for knowledge. This book will be a guide from which you can base your own knowledge and gain more. If you are interested in the information found in this book, continue learning through other advanced SQL books.

Working Through the Process

Many comprehensive books about any subject are difficult to continue due to their high requirement for previous knowledge and lack of examples. This book works through the process with you, and its sections are broken down to more effectively allow you places to stop and practice. Perfect practice makes perfect, and this book is designed to give you the knowledge to grow this information on your own. Follow the examples in the book and create your own database. Steps are listed to get you through the portions of this book that are difficult to understand, so you can navigate wisely.

The Ultimate Beginner's Step-by-Step Guide to Learn SQL Programming with Hands-On Projects is designed for beginners in mind, but more advanced techniques allow any reader to understand more about the SQL system and why it is still one of the top databases for business creation.

Chapter 1: Understanding SQL

SQL is a type of database that manipulates data in the form of tables and queries, a form of data collection whose original database design was initially invented in the 1980s. Since it's been so long since its invention, it may be difficult to believe that it hasn't become obsolete, but continued improvements and use has made it a go-to for many companies, and the future is bright for its continued usage.

Structured Query Language (SQL)

SQL, or *sequel* as it is also pronounced, is a database language that submits queries to a database management system that receives its data from the database. Simply put, SQL, also known as a Structured Query Language, acts as a communication system to translate large amounts of computer-stored data in a readable and manipulative form to effectively manage the information in a database.

Information is stored in a database, which is read by a database management system. A database may be a log of events and dates and the database management system holds this information in a program located on a computer. The dates and events in the database accessed by the database management system are then interpreted into formats easily manipulated by the language used to interpret the data, as is illustrated in Figure 1.1.

The advantages of using databases lies in their easy-retrieval

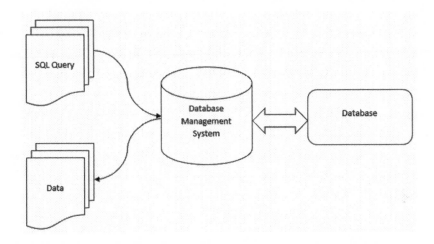

Figure 1.1: An SQL query processes through the database management service which accesses the database. The information is then sent back through the database management system to produce data.

setup. When inputting information for a company, a database organizes and retrieves information efficiently. The queries submitted from a database language like SQL are indexed and properly stored to manipulate in the future.

Databases

Databases store only information with no organization. Unlike paper methods, databases adjust with time, so the information is constantly evolving. Database knowledge is necessary to understand the communication between the programming language and database.

Relational and non-relational databases form the basis for data collection. Relational databases are organized into essential tables varying in size depending on the data points entered, splitting up data to related groups that are accessed directly through an SQL query. Non-relational databases, on the other hand, have an advantage in large data systems. Instead of table organizations, non-relational databases accommodate large amounts of data through minimal organization.

Non-Relational Database

A non-relational database is becoming more common due to its lack of excess mechanics. However, finding the correct information in a flood of data can be challenging, and finding data often takes a skilled programmer to develop pathways. For a system with a lot of data but lacking in complexity, the non-relational database fulfills the needs of a basic operating system.

Non-relational databases began as the hierarchical and network databases. The first, hierarchical, describes the descending order of important pathways. Just as a business might define their structure, the hierarchical method defines the largest file or structure and follows a flow-chart down to the details. Figure 1.2 illustrates this effect.

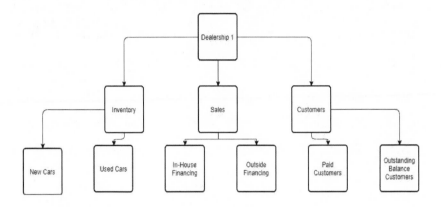

Figure 1.2: Model of the hierarchical system for a non-relational database.

Network non-relational databases were created to bypass some of the difficulties of the hierarchical system. Essentially, multiple files connected to a single source. For example, a car at a dealership is sold to a customer. The owner of the dealership, the salesman, and the customer are all linked to the product. Instead of large files of data dwindling down into bite-sized pieces of data, the relationship between a single file is displayed as a network of larger files. This is illustrated in Figure 1.3. On large scales, a non-relational database becomes exceptionally difficult to maintain.

While supporting this type of database does provide a simple rundown of the largest concepts to the smallest, it tends to fall apart in more complicated systems. Interactions between three or more are so-called mother/daughter relationships. Following the hierarchical system, when three or more dominant files interact with one another, their sub-files become entangled, and defining pathways becomes difficult.

The relational database connects files, linking them to one another and creating pathways to each other, providing a basis for more complex systems.

Relational Database

Relational databases provide a basis for related information. Imagine setting up a shop and writing down the customer information like name, address, date of sale, and item purchased. Now, imagine that the customer's address changed significantly, moving to a different city or state. Assuming that you are selling products that do not require payoffs, this information may not matter much. But what happens when you are selling a car and the length of payoff becomes much longer and more important?

Relational databases allow easy entry and organization into tables of related information. When an SQL query accesses data in a relational database, links with the

dataset connect with those who also satisfy the query. For

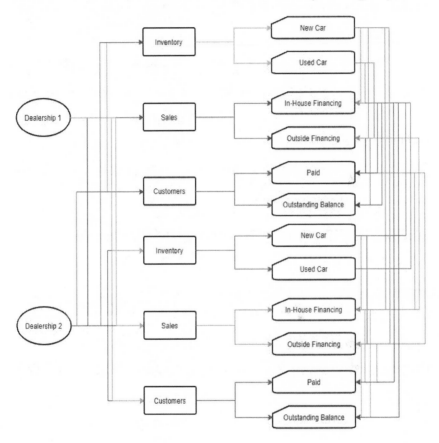

Figure 1.3: Model of a networked non-relational database. Multiple large files become tangled with possible intersecting files.

example, if John Bailey is our first customer, he may be assigned #1 – John Bailey. Information linked to his profile might include a mailing address, phone number, and credit card information. However, if John chooses to buy another product, that information, though not initially included in the information related to mailing address, phone number, or credit card information, will be linked to another row of his information in a relational database. If #2 – Barbara Brent becomes the next customer, her information is listed on the second row of information. When accessing data like names of customers who have bought an item from your shop, #1–- John Bailey and #2 – Barbara Brent will become easily accessible in the "person" information, effectively relating two customers with a single request: customer name file.

Each section of a relational database belongs to a table and is labeled according to its category. For example, customers listed in an SQL database are formed through a table assorted by name, addresses, and/or phone numbers, as illustrated in Figure 1.4. Each section of the database can be easily accessed through an SQL query, displaying each section individually or in related links.

Name	Phone Number	Address	Birthday
John Davis	555-676-878	123 Mulberry Way	10/2/1987
Barbara Brent	555-538-2846	135 Lincoln Blvd	7/31/1962
Francis Adams	555-937-3923	9875 Washington Way	9/26/2000
Matthew Richards	555-836-2946	4873 East St	8/30/1974
Tina Anderson	555-239-9275	9374 Main St	3/18/1948

Figure 1.4: Relational databases form tables.

Now, suppose that an owner of two dealerships liquidates one of the dealerships, deleting old files and condensing relevant information into the second dealership. The first dealership's information must be deleted from the second. Since both of the dealerships are owned by the same person, data overlaps. Relational integrity maintains an easy way to deal with this information and is defined as "the concept in which multiple database tables share a relationship based on the data stored in the tables, and that relationship must remain consistent" (Homan, 2014). A foreign key is required for both dealerships, providing a proverbial guardian of that information. When one dealership with an associated foreign key is deleted, its cascading file effect separates the data. The data listed on the first dealership is deleted through a cascading delete. The data associated with the first dealership, since it has been liquidated, requires deletion, and the relational integrity maintains the table structure of the second dealership.

SQL's relational database structure creates the perfect structure for linking information from one table to another, simply defining data by rows and columns. Each database is independent of the others, so tables formed in one database do not affect those in another.

Tables

A table is a combination of rows and columns with correlating information named after its description. The columns are a table's sorting system. Any of the data in a table is broken down into descriptors, which populate the headers for columns. For example, a table listing the customers for a dealership may contain columns listed by name, date of birth, customer street address, customer city, customer state, customer zip code, and date of visit. One column associated with one row gives a single data point for that customer. The rows that correspond to the associated columns are created through individual entries. Thus, tables grow larger as more information is entered.

All data listed under a single column contains only information related to the column name. A CITY column may contain data points such as NEW YORK, PITTSBURG, SALT LAKE CITY, or SAN DIEGO. All rows that have this information are assigned a TRUE value, which exists to show that the right information is displayed in both column and row.

Tables can be as small as you design, even including one column. Many SQL providers, however, usually impose some limit to the number of columns added to a table. However, if you find that your table is reaching the established limit, usually around 255 rows, it's time to think about splitting up your data anyway. Too much data in a table looks cluttered, and searching for and updating information can prove a hassle.

Tables can add as many rows as possible, and many allow you to add rows to a table until the data storage is filled, which can be upwards of 2 billion rows (Groff & Weinberg, 2010). Since data storage has advanced significantly, it's not uncommon to find SQL systems that exceed even that.

Primary Keys

Information added to any database is automatically assigned with an ID. Columns are the primary choice for primary keys, but what happens when there are two types of entries in the row columns? If New York is listed in Rows 2 and 3 but Washington D.C. is listed in Rows 1 and 4, the columns are no longer unique, making it impossible to differentiate which CITY specification to select in a search. For example, John Davis might receive an ID of 1, Barbara Brent may receive 2, and so on. The primary key also differentiates data from one customer to the next. Francis Adams's ID of 3 ties her name, phone number, address, and birthdate to her unique identifier. Since Francis and John may live in the same city, that location identifier can no longer be used, and another takes its place, like the unique phone numbers.

It is not only possible but common that two columns may be set up as primary keys. Two stores may get their merchandise from the same manufacturer, but each product has a unique ID. The combination of the two sets of data creates a unique list. Any identifiers for products listed in a store's table may be uniquely identified by the combination of the two columns.

The name "relational database" comes from the term relation, which describes unique tables. Tables that have unique rows are called *relations* and were named from the mathematical description (Groff & Weinberg, 2010). As SQL grew over the past few decades, its ways of identifying unique phrases and data developed to a more sophisticated system. SQL now, unlike previous versions, allows for the navigation through keys by providing its own.

Foreign Keys

Information stored in a table has unique rows, and redundant data is discarded. To ensure a database that can break down tables and prevent them from creating large, inefficient monsters, data can be replicated in more than one table. The breakdown of a business may include a table of inventory in a dealership. The inventory table is broken down into sections such as VIN, mileage, make, model, stock number, and year. Each entry is unique, and, since mileage, make, model, and year may be the same for two separate vehicles, the VIN and/or stock number may be our primary keys. Once sold, the vehicle then belongs to the table marked as SOLD VEHICLES, and other connections are made to relate it with other tables. The customer table, for instance, looks completely different. The customer's information may show home city, street address, zip code, home phone number, and birthdate. When he or she buys a vehicle, however, the vehicle's primary key (in our example VIN and/or stock number) is then placed in the customer table.

The basic concept of a foreign key is identifying the relationship of one uniquely identifying column with another. Since both the vehicle and customer tables hold a car's VIN, we can relate the information from one table to the other. Foreign keys are the basis for joins, which we will explain in more detail in Chapter 6.

Brandon Cooper

Summary

SQL (Structured Language Query) is the language used to communicate with a relational database management system (RDMS), which receives data from a database. SQL, a language that communicates with the database through queries, allows users to manipulate data within a relational database.

A non-relational database connects information through either a networked or hierarchical model. Though able to handle large amounts of data, neither of these models are preferred because they cannot handle many connections.

A relational database, which is managed with SQL, connects data through tables. These tables are organized by columns, and each data entry is added to the table through a new row. Each row is unique, and several billion rows are usually allowed when constructing each table. Primary and foreign keys identify unique data and allow for connection through the database.

Chapter 2: Creating a Database and Data Entry

This chapter explores data manipulation in one or multiple databases through SQL queries. Setting up a database, as you may expect, is the first step. Though there are several relational database management systems that will create an SQL server, we will focus on MySQL.

Creating a Database

Creating a database through a relational database management system (RDMS) is one of the first steps in setting up an SQL system. RDMSs like MySQL, Oracle, and MS Access provide the platforms for creating your own database.

To set up your own database with MySQL, follow these steps:

1. Navigate to http://dev.mysql.com/downloads. Since we are working with the latest database, select the newest model, usually listed as MySQL Installer for Windows.

2. Select the option listed as Windows (x86, 32-bit), MSI Installer.

3. Select "Run" when the popup asks "Do you want to run or save this file?"

4. Accept all installer agreements.

5. Select "Install."

6. When the installer completes, select "Configure the MySQL Server now."

7. Select the boxes marked "Install as Window Service" and "Include Bin Directory in Windows Path."

8. Execute.

Many RDMSs provide options to create databases with commands as easy as typing in CREATE DATABASE followed by the name you've chosen for your database. Deleting the database is just as simple in MySQL with the command DROP DATABASE, but this should never be used lightly. This will destroy your database and lose all the data included. To be safe, it's best to not use this at all.

Databases also require unique names since multiple databases with the same name will cause confusion in the pathways (Colby & Wilton, 2005). Naming databases for divisions in your company is a good start to set up multiple databases. Consider the example listed above about the two car dealerships. Assuming you are using the same SQL service and RDMS for both and the dealerships, located across town from each other, have the same name. If both databases share the same name, SQL queries will confuse the information, making both databases obsolete with confused information.

Just as stated earlier, creating tables is the basis of an SQL database. Table names are equally as important in those databases as they define the access points for relational databases. Before information is added to a database, master tables are created to provide bases for incoming data.

Creating and Applying Data

Most databases allow views of tables, but without specialized software, entering large amounts of data is time-consuming and ineffective. Using an SQL language to adapt information in tables once they are created within the database. With tables inserted, the next step is to insert data.

Setting Up the Database

Creating a design for your database is the first step in database creation. Information displayed in your database ultimately changes the layout of the program. Tables designed to show a customer's information versus a table created to reflect only the selling of a product will look differently in the database. Ultimately, the tables in your database must reflect the information listed there. Poor design may include placing too much information in one table and not splitting the information in two.

For example, creating a table with information linking a salesperson to the cars he or she sells requires a unique identifier. Every salesperson with a unique identifier, like 123, to prevent redundancy. Keeping every salesperson in a non-relational database linked to their sales using a spreadsheet may duplicate information, leading to possible incorrect commission or misinformation about the cars sold. However, unique identifiers linking a salesperson to his or her table within an SQL database gives you all the information for that salesperson.

Normalization is the process of separating data into readable and accessible tables that make data manipulation easy. Creating tables that are accessed through unique identifiers is the first step of normalization, also known as the *first normal form*.

First Normal Form

The first normal form consists of the information we've already covered. Start by setting up tables with named columns and defined data. Normalize the data by keeping track of the data and entering it only once. Duplicate columns make it impossible for the RDMS to determine which set of data to pull.

A table set up with a car's information with two columns expressing the car's mileage creates confusion in the system.

Just as you may write down the information on paper and write down the duplication, if an employee comes back to the data the next day, without knowing which mileage is correct ahead of time, he or she will not know which mileage to display on an information sheet about the car.

Splitting the data in multiple tables prevents the loss of data. For instance, putting meeting times, notes, and people attending into different tables prevents *deletion anomaly*. This applies when a category, like people attending the meeting, is deleted and all data is deleted, including the information you want to keep (Colby & Wilton, 2005). Linking the data includes those unique identifiers tied to each table but avoids deleting other information.

Second Normal Form

When all information is entered with careful regard taken to prevent duplication, the next step is to create tables that break down information further. For example, when entering information about a car dealership's inventory, the table may display just the vehicle names, VINs, and dates purchased. The next step is to break down the information of the cars further in another table connected to the first by a unique identifier.

A 2006 Dodge Charger will have an identifier different than a 2019 Toyota Camry. All cars are listed in the first table holding all cars listed for the dealership. Creating a second table splits information into a refined category, like current inventory and sold vehicles. Accessing the information through an SQL query recognizes unique identifiers, pulling on the information requested.

There are additional normal forms, but for the sake of this book, we will refrain. Adding too many layers in normal forms gums up fast data processes, making the database slow and reducing efficiency.

Retrieve Data

The essentials of an SQL database start with retrieving data. After all, after data is entered into the database, the only way to make changes or even find information is to utilize SQL queries to retrieve information. Every command discussed in this chapter depends on the SQL language's ability to retrieve data.

The SELECT command is the essential first step in retrieving data. The data entered in a table is dependent on the number of columns and rows. SQL's SELECT query asks for all the information listed in a row. Additional commands such as WHERE, FROM, INTO, and HAVING determine where to retrieve the information.

The FROM Clause

The FROM clause is essential in its definition of tabular structure. Databases require this clause to determine the locations of tables inside. The FROM clause essentially points us to the bigger picture. Just as discussed previously, more than one table may contain a single set of data. For example, a table containing only salespeople may be linked to a table containing data for a single salesperson. The FROM clause differentiates from where the information is collected. The table Salespeople may contain the same information as Salespeople Group A, but the distinguishing FROM sends an SQL query to the right table more efficiently.

The WHERE Clause

WHERE sends the SQL query to the right column and row, and its subsequent order defines where the information is pulled. Like the FROM clause, WHERE specifies a location, this time within a table itself. The WHERE clause shuffles through information and determines which information is where based on three conditions:

- When an SQL query returns the result TRUE, the information searched for is located in that row and table. This response determines that the results are available in that row.

- The FALSE result shows that the information is not available in that row, excluding it from searches.

- When NULL is displayed, the database returns an unknown value. In this case, too, the data is excluded.

The INTO Clause

The SQL INTO query essentially creates new information. New information is put into a table through a row addition. Information listed must include all data associated with the columns inside the table. For example, a table listing famous actors may include columns such as name, first television appearance, first breakthrough movie, and style of acting. Adding an actor, such as Brad Pitt, would require adding his data regarding all these subjects.

The HAVING Clause

Similar to the WHERE clause, the HAVING clause determines which data is included in a search. TRUE, FALSE, and NULL responses equally define if information is located in the table, just as the WHERE clause specifies.

All of these clauses direct SQL queries to retrieve different types of information, either finding, adding, or deleting data. For example, consider our example in Chapter 1. Paperwork concerning the sale of his vehicle and the sales tax owed to the state is required. The sale was completed two months ago, and it is difficult to remember everything required to send to the state. The required SQL query to retrieve this information is in the SELECT query. Using the WHERE clause, we can easily select the table that includes the information, making the search more efficient.

Retrieving information from tables is the first step to data manipulation. Inserting, updating, and deleting data are some of the most basic ways to create these tables.

Summarize Data

The SQL language not only allows you to access and retrieve data, but it also allows a summary of that data. Summarizing data finds the average of data from a table. Suppose you are looking for the employee with the best sales numbers for the year. Instead of using 12 different tables to find whose average is better, we will use the GROUP BY command, effectively telling the database which section of information needs gathering for summary. This is a brief summary of summarizing data, and we will return to it when we discuss grouping data.

Insert Data

Just as you'd expect, the command for inserting data is simple. The INSERT INTO command directly pulls information from your command into database tables arranged by columns and rows.

INSERT INTO table_name (column_names) VALUES (data_values)

Multiple column names and data values are possible in the command if entered with a comma separation. Each successive entry into the table will produce additional rows with column value entries. For example, inserting data in columns named CatagoryNumber and Category of the table named Movie Types is done through the following commands.

INSERT INTO Movie_Types (CategoryNumber, Category) VALUES (1, Horror);

INSERT INTO Movie_Types (CategoryNumber, Category) VALUES (2, Comedy);

INSERT INTO Movie_Types (CategoryNumber, Category) VALUES (3, Adventure);

When inserting data, it's possible to remit the columns by simply typing

INSERT INTO table_name VALUES (data_values);

and the RDMS will fill in the rest (Colby & Wilton, 2005). Additional information, such as dates, may be subject to the SQL term used. The United States, the United Kingdom, and many other countries differ in date formatting, so creating a database that accommodates many adaptations for every country is impractical. MySQL orders their date as year/month/day. As such, entering a birthday for Joe Smith will read 1987/12/5.

Update Data

It's often the case that, as time goes on, data changes. For example, an address for a customer may change when he or she moves to a different state. Instead of throwing out the table, the best option is to use the UPDATE command to simply change the address without changing any other information in a customer's table. The WHERE clause defines where this change takes place. Sending an SQL query regarding a specific table refined by column name defines the location for the updated data. The following command is the basis for any updated data.

UPDATE table_name

SET column_name = value

WHERE condition

For John Davis, in the example listed in Chapter 1, his information located in the Customers table is located through the command

UPDATE Customers

SET

Address = "8435 Tolkein Rd"

`WHERE = CustomerID 1`

This command, though very simple, is important to get right. If we search for information about CustomerID 1 and more than one set of data corresponds to that unique identifier, data corruption is possible. Getting the WHERE clause wrong when identifying locations can also cause data corruption. When programming the database, keep the unique identifiers in mind.

The Logic Operators

The commands AND OR logically connect two independent pieces of information. Connecting these two commands is easy to understand due to its parallels with the English language. Using AND or modifies two sets of data with the WHERE operator. Updating data through these commands is easier through these commands.

Delete Data

Once again, the WHERE operator is essential in selecting data to delete. Just like the UPDATE operator, we can delete more than one line of data through the AND or operators, and excluding the WHERE operator, all rows are deleted (Beaulieu, 2009). The DELETE command deletes entire tables, rows, or columns when appropriately selected. The general commands for deletion for names, columns, and rows are given by

```
DELETE table_name
```

```
DELETE FROM table_name
```

```
WHERE column_name
```

```
DELETE FROM table_name
```

```
WHERE column_name = value
```

Deletion using an SQL query finds the same information in the same way that the SELECT command finds information. SQL queries effectively select the necessary data and retrieve the information before deletion. The database then reorders itself accommodate the deletion of the row.

Suppose Barbara Brent had a falling out at the car dealership, and due to lack of payments, the car dealer wants to completely delete the customer's information with the car's return to the dealership. To delete Barbara Brent's information from our database, we use the command

```
DELETE FROM Customers
```

```
WHERE CustomerID = 2
```

Her information, found through the definition of customer data, deletes her row. Francis Adams's information, previously CustomerID = 3, takes Barbara Brent's place.

Alter Data

When altering the definition of data already entered into the table, use the ALTER TABLE command. When creating a business, it's not only possible but probable that you'll need to adjust information stored in your databases. The ALTER TABLE request selects the table, column, and row that needs adjusting by utilizing the *auto-increment* option on your SQL server. The *auto-increment* option effectively creates an additional column to the end of every table.

Sorting Data

Ordering information after it has been put into the database shouldn't be difficult. The ORDER BY clause allows the movement of data in columns and rows. Initial data may not be entered in any particular order, which makes the ORDER BY clause essential to maintaining an orderly database. When using a database for a long time, like for a long-lasting business, data shuffles about and new information takes precedence to old.

Ascending data is the primary format for initial raw data. Tables showing profit margins per city, for instance, will display the largest amounts first, as is displayed in Figure 2.1. Tables that have data with multiple sets of data essentially forming a "tie" show no particular order. Using an SQL query using the ORDER BY clause effectively allows you to choose which order you prefer. Changing that order begins with an SQL query subjected to a command such as DESC, which will change the direction of data per city, a useful tool to focus on the amount of sales needed to save or reduce monetary flow in that area.

Single Table Query

Single table queries are generally the easiest. All the information for a single dealership's salespeople, for example, may exist in a single table (though we do not suggest that all information should be confined to one table). Looking for a salesperson within the system requires the use of this salesperson's table. Search for the number of this salesperson through a single query. According to James R. Groff and Paul N. Weinberg's complete guide to SQL, they suggest the following steps to query using the SELECT statement.

1. Use the FROM clause to navigate to the correct table.

2. If you use the WHERE clause, implement it for every row of the table and sort it by the TRUE, FALSE, and NULL statements. Discard those that return the results FALSE and NULL.

3. For every remaining row, sort the results to produce a row that has all the TRUE statements. For every column statement, use the correct column name and

the associated column ID to navigate through the TRUE results.

4. If SELECT DISTINCT is queried (which is defined by unique entries), use the independent rows and delete any duplicates.

5. Use the ORDER BY clause to order the table as specified (2010).

Defining the order of each table determines which column will be affected and which rows will sort according to a set design. For example, when searching for the phone number of salespeople, identifying the column responsible for holding phone numbers may be more vital than knowing their addresses. In this case, sorting the information from ascending order by phone numbers listed may be the best use of space in your database.

Consider the most efficient way to order your database. Likely, placing the salesperson ID in conjunction with their number of sales may be more efficient than tying the salesperson's information with the name of every customer that is a prospect for a sale.

There are various ways to order a table, and many of them are simple. Simply putting in data does not provide the most efficient way to retrieve data. Sorting in descending order, via expressions, and via name placeholders are some of the most common ways to order data.

Ascending vs Descending Order

SQL tables are automatically set up in ascending order, so why would you want to create a table that was ordered from bottom to top? Using this technique is often paired with knowing top accounts. For example, if New York City has multiple car dealerships but New Jersey's fewer car dealerships are receiving a larger profit in all dealerships combined, knowing the largest accounts will give you greater insight into which state, city, or dealership needs more attention.

Choosing an ascending order may provide easier calculations. Instead of knowing the top numbers for business entries, knowing the average number of people that work at a specific dealership may give you more information through an ascending order. This way, it's easier to decipher which employees have been there longer and how much turnover may be associated with your business.

Expressions

Sometimes finding the numbers associated with the customer IDs are not as efficient as sorting your customers through their social security numbers. Plugging in an employee's social security number will group employee numbers in numerical order, making finding that information easier.

Numeric Placeholders

Perhaps the order to use least is the numeric placeholder. This is in reference to finding data by column numbers. For example, say the first and third customers' information is the most valuable to the dealership since they each have large accounts. Using ORDER BY as a means to locate these two accounts at the top of the list places them in a high-priority location.

Because relational database tables are constantly in flux due to new information and deletion of old data, ordering data by this method is to be used sparingly, if at all. Use this ordering, instead, as a temporary method to keep important information at the top of your table.

Single table queries are easier to define. Once multiple queries are used to define the order of sequences, the queries become more complex. When first learning basic SQL queries, adjust only single tables to become more adept at understanding the basic clauses for data manipulation.

Summary

Creating a database requires unique information that is set up to prevent repetition also called normalization. Design your database with function in mind. Create tables that are easy to access and are not overloaded with information. Break your tables down into bite-sized pieces that allow you to easily access details and connect them with one another through queries.

Retrieving data starts with the SELECT command. Access data from anywhere by requiring the database to access the information using the FROM, WHERE, INTO, and HAVING clauses. The FROM clause specifies a table location and is commonly used to gather data. The WHERE clause is often used in data manipulation, including inserting, updating, and deleting data. The INTO clause is common in inserting and updating data. The HAVING clause, similar to the FROM and WHERE clauses, specifies what information is included in a search.

Sorting data is done through common commands such as ASC ( ), DESC ( ), the characters that make up worded expressions, and numeric placeholders such as listed rows. Expressions, characters expressed in letters and phrases, and numeric placeholders, like customer and employee IDs, guide queries to correct tables, columns, and rows.

Chapter 3: Data Manipulation

We have already discussed some of the most basic types of data manipulation, such as SELECT, INSERT, DELETE, and UPDATE, but what are the basic functions within an SQL system? The basics of data manipulation start with basic math, and this language is applicable to all SQL systems.

SQL Arithmetic

Just like any other language, arithmetic is the basis for systematic understanding. Numeric lists and queries form the basis for any SQL system. However, when it comes to the type of arithmetic available in SQL, the options are fairly limited. That said, we'll start with the most basic of arithmetic functions that apply in any database: multiplication (*), division (/), addition (+), and subtraction (-). All arithmetic follows the same order of operation as basic mathematics, so a code multiplying characters by three and adding two will follow the same suit.

Other mathematical entries are also included in SQL, though you may not expect to see these used as often. Using these tools, just as you would mathematics, creates a database easier to manipulate.

The Absolute Function

Often seen as ABS (), the absolute function behaves as it would in mathematics. Determining the total sales when cooking the numbers for the second store in a long chain of stores may require use of the ABS () function. Sales within the chain depend on the flux in orders, and finding the difference in the average of sales from every store in the chain gives you the information about the functionality of the chain and lets you know which stores show the most drastic change in averages.

The common code for finding the absolute value is given by

ABS (x)

The Power Function

Just as you've learned in school, the power function raises a function to an arbitrary amount, determining how many times that function must multiply itself. Expressing the power function in SQL takes two factors: the initial function and the power to which it is raised.

POWER (expression, power_raise_to)

But why would you want to use the power function? Often, the use for this function lies in the easy calculation of exponential growth.

The Square Root Function

Like the power function, the square root function applies to an exponential. However, this data produces a power that is listed as 1 divided by the power. Again, the basics for executing the SQRT () function is through the square root of the function only, since the cubed root, fourth root, and so on are rarely used.

SQRT (expression)

String Functions

Each character entered into a database has a corresponding line of 0s and 1s, just as you'd expect for any binary system. String functions relate to alphabet characters lined up in a proverbial string. For example, the entry, "I can see it", would be an example for a string function, though these words in particular hold no meaning unless they are imputed into a meaningful arrangement in SQL. String functions such as the names of people or places are examples of string functions with meaning in an SQL system. Searching and manipulating data that correspond to these arrangements is the beginning of understanding string functions.

The SUBSTRING () Function

Like subqueries, which we will explain more in-depth in Chapter 4, substring functions allow you to search for small sets of string functions. Data is found through substrings by associating each character with a number and using that number to define where your data lies. For example, the phrase WORD PRESS is broken down into numbered sections, giving us Table 3.1. Each character is numbered by its position in the phrase, so to find a particular string of data, the code would read as follows.

SUBSTRING (string, start_character_position, length_of_string)

This means that if you are looking to find data on WORD PRESS, our example above, we would use the code

SUBSTRING (WORD PRESS, 1, 9).

Case Conversion Functions

Just as easy as it sounds, conversion functions such as UPPER () and LOWER () convert strings from upper case to lower and vice versa. Possible uses for these functions include renaming the customers in a table. Though this may seem inconsequential, as databases become more advanced, case-sensitivity becomes more of a factor. Therefore, expressing functions in either upper or lower case would yield the codes:

UPPER (Lastname);

LOWER (Lastname);

TRIM () Functions

TRIM () functions trim unwanted characters from a string. Though snatching a few characters off the end of a phrase may not seem worthwhile, deleting spaces in between large strings can provide more efficient space in your database. The commands LTRIM () and RTRIM () remove characters from the left and right respectively.

LENGTH () Functions

The LENGTH () function displays the length of any string. Substring functions require the length of the string in their commands, and the LENGTH () function provides that information without unnecessary slogging through the data. LENGTH () can also be used in conjunction with the SUBSTRING () command to use clauses such as UPPER () and LOWER () to change information within the database.

The Date Function

Times and dates vary depending on the country or area, so it is no surprise that SQL databases would have its own style of dates and times. American time reads as month/day/year, the

British record dates as day.month.year, and the Japanese express dates as year-month-day. In the SQL language, the date and time typically follow the style of the Japanese and are inserted as year-month-day. However, variations to date and time styles are supported within the RDMS as time stamps.

Functions	Returns
CAST	Convert a value to a specified data type
CONVERT	Convert data by a named conversion function
CURRENT_DATE CURRENT_TIME	Current date and time
CURRENT_TIME_STAMP	Specification of the current style of date and time
EXTRACT	Specified part of a DATETIME value
POSITION	Target strings appears in source string
TRANSLATION	Translated string through translation function

SQL databases cannot record durations, but they still have unique ways of manipulating the information from entered data. For example, a command that looks for the resignation date plus two weeks would have its own coding.

RESIGNATION_DATE + 14 DAYS

SQL keeps track of the final day of each employee through the manipulation of the date function. Extracting information about customers is also handy and is readily available in SQL systems by using the SELECT command.

SELECT   DateofSale,   DAY   (DateofSale),   MONTH (DateofSale), YEAR (DateofSale)

    FROM Purchases

Built-In Functions

Many SQL databases have their own language concerning general data manipulation, but most styles, like ORACLE12, MySQL, and PostgreSQL, have the same built-in commands. Here is a list of some of the most common examples and their uses.

Summary

Just as everyday practices and paper and pen companies must use basic mathematical skills to manipulate data, so SQL must use the same methods to affect its data. Simple functions like the absolute value function, the power function, and the square root function play an integral role in developing a database that manipulates data best. Mathematical functions within the system allow for adjusted views of data and provide possible adjustments to data to determine the present and future of the company.

String functions, also known as functions that correspond with non-numeric characters, are essential to keeping data in an organized state within a database. While numeric data is also necessary for a well-organized database, characters and phrases within the system allow for more accurate descriptions of columns within a table. The SUBSTRING ( ) function, case conversion functions, TRIM ( ) function, and LENGTH ( ) function all serve to manipulate the data within a string for easier access in the database.

Built-in functions, such as the date function, allow for easier transitions into the SQL language. The simple queries listed in the table above provide easy access to data within tables.

Chapter 4: Subqueries

We have already discussed multiple types of clauses, including HAVING, WHERE, INTO, and FROM. But what is the definition of a subquery? A subquery is a query within a query, starting from a basic query, such as SELECT, and narrowing data manipulation even further. Developing the techniques to create subqueries is essential to easily maintain an SQL database.

Subqueries are queries contained within parentheses subject to its parent query. These queries are distinguished by primary keys. Daughter queries are described through foreign keys. For example, SELECT MIN (account) is an example of a subquery. Subqueries are discarded after a command completes. According to Alan Bleaulieu, "When the [initial query] has finished executing, the data returned by any subqueries is discarded, making a subquery act like a temporary table with statement scope (meaning that the server frees up any memory allocated to the subquery results after the SQL statement has finished execution)" (2009). Subqueries make SQL commands easier to navigate, and they save time. It's so much easier to execute commands in one query rather than two.

Types of Subqueries

The two types of subqueries are defined by how they interact with data around them. For instance, *non-correlated queries* do not reference previous queries, where *correlated queries* do. Each type of query has a specific type of clause applied it depending on its connection to data.

Non-Correlated Subqueries

Unless you plan to update or delete data, the non-correlated subquery is the most common to use. Non-correlated queries may look like an insert statement, which return tables with columns. These commands do not require using information in an already-established table but are more common as creating data queries. Non-correlated queries may utilize equality or inequality signs and are often defined as scalar subqueries. The example below shows this.

SELECT City

FROM New_York

WHERE Store1 > (SELECT SUM (QUOTA)

FROM Salesdata

WHERE Salespeople = Office)

This query opens accounts for New York within store one and selects the quota from all salespeople in the office. The information is independent of actions in other tables, as the data is pulled from information only in Store1. The whittling down effect seen here is the primary purpose of a subquery. Instead of sending a query, writing down the information in a table from the database, remembering that information, and then posting a query that will reach that data through multiple queries, the non-correlated query takes care of this in one easy action. The example above uses many clauses to reach the data, but subqueries can be as easy or as difficult as necessary to achieve the end goal. A query may use any and all clauses (such as SELECT, FROM, HAVING, GROUP BY, and WHERE) to find and alter data.

The IN Operator

When one query displays more than one row of data, it is impossible to use equality signs to compare the two, but functions, such as the operator IN, to find selective data. Using the following query shows how the IN operator can return data.

```
SELECT City, Name, StationID

FROM Station

WHERE name IN ('Outlet', 'Brooklyn');
```

IN creates two possible locations for the data required. The data for city, name, and station ID are all found in the results. Therefore, even if there is more than one row of data, the information will show in the results. Results with multiple points of data effectively filter out useless information. Along with the IN operator, the NOT IN operator shows all data outside the stated conditions.

The ALL Operator

While the IN operator shows TRUE and FALSE results within given parameters, the ANY and ALL operators allow for comparison from one data set to another. Both effectively test data for quantified results. Data values entered into the SQL database are compared with data found in a specified table's column whose results are produced by a subquery (Groff & Weinberg, 2010). The ANY and ALL operators are essentially tests for data entered.

The ALL test requires equality functions, such as <, >, =, <>, etc. Suppose we look for employees and managers. To calculate this, we use the ALL operator in conjunction with employee IDs not equal to manager IDs.

SELECT EmployeeID, name, title

FROM Employee

WHERE   EmployeeID   <>   ALL   (SELECT Employee_ManagerID

    FROM Employee

    WHERE Employee_ID IS NOT NULL)

The code seems like a handful, but it actually gives very useful information. Employees are effectively compared to managers, and the resulting information tells us exactly which employees supervise others. To understand what each result means, we'll delve in deeper.

When an ALL query returns with an empty column, all information yields the result TRUE, which means all comparisons give the same results. When the subquery returns a column with only true statements, the columns are essentially identical. For example, comparing data of ordered items from Store 1 to Store 2 may be identical if both stores sell roughly the same amount of materials. If the two stores are on opposite sides of the same mall, both stores may receive roughly the same number of patrons, giving similar results.

If the query results in one FALSE, all data in the column are considered FALSE, which will reflect in the results. If a query returns NULL for any data in the columns while returning TRUE in all of the other columns, the comparison test results in NULL data, as some information listed in the column is incorrect (Groff & Weinberg, 2010). The ALL query reduces the amount of information by not accepting only some TRUE data.

If this seems complicated, it is. Many choose not to use the ALL test as it is difficult to understand, but it is useful in deciphering information requiring the comparison of all data.

The ANY Test

Like the ALL test, queries using the ANY test involve inequalities. Two sets of data are compared with each other, but instead of all results requiring identical data to produce TRUE, any of the data that result in TRUE for the ANY test will provide TRUE results. Suppose a company is looking for data regarding any salesperson that exceeded $20,000 in commission over the last month. The ANY test determines all people who fulfill this requirement.

```
SELECT Name

FROM Salespeople

WHERE 20000.00 < ANY (SELECT AMOUNTS

                       FROM CARSALES

                          WHERE    Salespeople    =
Employee_num)
```

All salespeople who fall into this category will be listed in the results. $20,000 is the point at which all employees must reach to be included. Depending on the SQL provider, the SOME clause may yield the same results. It is best to practice this before including large amounts of data. According to Groff and Weinberg, the system must follow these rules when entering ANY queries:

- If the column returned from an ANY query is empty, all information is returned as FALSE. The empty table indicates that there is no connection between the two columns.

- If the column returns any value that is TRUE, the entire system is TRUE.

- If all the data values return FALSE, there is no salvageable material. All information in the resulting column proves that there is no connection between the two sets of data and the comparison test fails.

- If none of the results list TRUE or FALSE but return with NULL, the test is inconclusive. NULL means that the information listed in the column is unknown, and you can conclusively state that the information stated may or may not be true (2010).

Correlated Subqueries

Correlated subqueries are dependent on the queries that come before them. Every row that may include information relevant to future data must be included in a correlated subquery. For example, using the SELECT query, we'll find the information regarding customers from two accounts.

```
SELECT CustomerID, Cutomer_type, Customer_city
FROM Customers
WHERE 2 = (SELECT COUNT (NAME)
        FROM Account1
```

WHERE 1.CustomerID = 2.CustomerID

The query harkens back to the initial post through 2.CustomerID, making it a correlated subquery. All information found in the final WHERE clause compares 1.CustomerID to 2.CustomerID. Each clause is dependent on the last.

The EXISTS Operator

Correlated subqueries are used for variable ranges and equalities, but the most common operator is the EXISTS operator. This operator is in the correlated subquery section because it depends on the relationship between the initial query with its corresponding subquery. Any subquery with the operator EXISTS closely resembles the initial SELECT query.

If the query produces any rows in a table, the operator EXISTS is TRUE. Since the operator is highly expansive, any answer in the field that does not provide a FALSE statement proves that the information exists.

Summary

Subqueries are essential to the smooth movement of a database. Insert queries are examples of non-correlated subqueries. These queries require no manipulation of data to perform accurately. The IN, ALL, and ANY tests and operators compare two types of data, and each can be included in a query without disrupting existing data.

Correlated subqueries correspond to already-existing tables that affect other parts of the system once entered. Updating and deleting data are forms of correlated subqueries that rely on the query to manipulate data.

Chapter5:Grouping, Aggregating, and Filtering Data

At its most basic level, an SQL database holds only the information that is required in each table. Each search result for a customer's information may show different results for the different departments in your business. For example, accounting may need the overall payments received by John Davis, while the sales department only needs to know how many sales applied to him. Grouping data is a means to differentiate which data is applicable to each person. Aggregation is the summary of all data. Using the GROUP BY command to separate information allows the possibility for aggregation. Grouping supplies the information and orders it in groups for a particular record, and aggregation summarizes the data within that group (Colby & Wilton, 2005). Through grouping, the same relational database can hold the same information for everyone, but the results are made applicable to different people.

Understanding Grouping

Let us consider a business with four employees accessing the till. Finding out which of your employees accessed the till at 6pm. Assuming the business has only recently opened up and the employees that access the till are only available at only one time during the day, it's easy to find out who had access at that time.

Grouping Data

Now, what if the dealership has grown to ten times the size it was at the time of opening. There are now five to ten people at the till at any time of day, and it's important to find out who has had the most access. Though we can still use the employee table to find out who has access and when, if you are looking for that time exactly over the course of several months, the work can become tedious. This is the perfect time to begin grouping data.

The GROUP BY Clause

If a table is organized by the employee ID, we can find which employees worked at that time and organize them accordingly. For example, consider Jonah, Ruth, and Everest, employees that work the same evening shift. Each employee in the SQL database has a unique identifier tied with his or her name. Suppose Jonah, Ruth, and Everest, respectively, have employee ID numbers 4, 8, 20. The command to group data regarding only these three people is

SELECT open_EmployeeID

FROM Employee_List

`GROUP BY open_EmployeeID = 4, 8, 20`

As a result, a row is created for every employee ID selected. As you'll notice, the SELECT and GROUP BY options have the same columns, and this is by no accident. The RDMS requires a selection to determine which data to group. The SELECT clause breaks down which table is accessed, and then the GROUP BY clause allows for column manipulation.

The HAVING Clause

Just like the WHERE clause, the HAVING clause demands that data is selected. The query is essentially a searching condition. For example, when searching a group by state names, the GROUP BY clause is followed by the HAVING clause, narrowing the results to a single item, like total profits. Consider our example listed above. Suppose the business is doing so well that it has expanded to multiple states. This is great, but how do we tell which store in each state has the best sales without mucking through thousands of accounts? The example below is a possible query.

`SELECT open_EmployeeID`

`FROM Sales`

`GROUP BY open_EmployeeID`

`HAVING SUM(AMOUNT) > 50000.00`

The HAVING clause restricts the locations listed to sums larger than $50,000, and the SELECT clause shows the averages of the entries that satisfy that condition.

Though the HAVING clause is almost always accompanied by the GROUP BY clause, it is not always required. If the HAVING clause is alone, SQL automatically assumes that the data from which to select is found in the SELECT listing. Though you might never see this format in practice, consider it in the future.

Grouping Restrictions

Unfortunately, though there are many benefits to grouping, there are command restrictions involved also. Grouped clauses must connect to actual data in table columns given in the FROM command. Queries must also include all data from each row. This means that, when using SELECT, all columns listed must have data points.

The NULL Dilemma

Grouping is an excellent way for multiple people to access different information in the same database. But what happens when NULL is one of the results in grouping? When entering a query for a comparison between two NULL values, SQL becomes confused and is often unable to decipher between the two, resulting in a new grouping with the definition of NULL.

When grouping information, SQL will then create two groups: one that groups all information that returns the result TRUE, and the other is a group within containing only NULL results.

If the number of columns in the NULL groups equal those in the TRUE groups with the same information located in the non-NULL results, SQL will combine the groups together in the same row group (Groff & Weinberg, 2010). Test practice how your SQL database works with data before you begin adding large quantities of data.

Aggregating Data

The next step is to aggregate data. Information is summarized by selecting large amounts of data and utilizing the COUNT () clause. Any column may be selected in the COUNT () command, which is located by the SELECT clause. The COUNT (*) command summarizes all data. Selecting a column with the COUNT (*) for the number of states in the United States may yield 51, but the COUNT (States) command will only yield 50. Why is that the case? The asterisk counts all rows in the column, while the States query only returns information for which the result is not NULL. In this case, Puerto Rico may have been entered into the system, but it does not qualify as a full-fledged state, so it returns NULL.

Following our example, aggregating through an SQL query summarizes the data for each employee, logging the number of rows associated with each employee that opens the register at exactly 6pm.

```
SELECT open_EmployeeID, COUNT(*) how_many
FROM Employee_List
GROUP BY open_EmployeeID = 4, 8, 20
```

All GROUP BY commands should follow the FROM or WHERE clause. The GROUP BY query corresponds to locations inside tables, defining changing in columns. It is possible to include more than one GROUP BY query, separated by commas, just as you would for a SELECT query.

Filtering Data

When starting out, creating the data for a database may involve frequent deletion and restarts. Grouping all data in one place may seem like the best option at the beginning of MySQL trials, but that changes when large amounts of data are stored in the database and only some of that information requires reworking.

The WHERE clause, as we've seen previously, is highly adaptable to any query, and its use is common. The HAVING and FROM clauses also specify how data is filtered. Each of these clauses are considered *filtering* clauses. Just like a funnel, the more information we put into a query, the more the information is refined. All clauses, except INSERT, can be effectively filtered by using the WHERE clause.

Parentheses

When using the WHERE clause, parentheses are vital in separating data for evaluation. For example, when searching for a customer's name within a database, parentheses differentiate the information found in both the same and other tables. An SQL query may specify the table selected, or it may specify the information to be found.

SELECT MemberID

FROM City_name

WHERE end_date IS NULL

     AND (title = title_name OR start_date)

The WHERE clause effectively cuts down the information into smaller bits so the RDMS can narrow down the search.

The NOT Operator

As we've described before, using filtering clauses such as WHERE, INTO, FROM, and HAVING narrow down the search for selected data. The NOT operator, however, displays data with no correlation to its clause. For example, just as in the example above, suppose we search for members whose

IDs are not associated with a title or start date of three months ago. A code may look something like this:

```
SELECT MemberID
FROM City_name
WHERE end_date IS NULL
    AND NOT (title = title_name OR start_date)
```

This information is handy when many data points are entered. If the members in this scenario had just received a membership but had not earned the rewards associated with it, this system would provide insight into which members should be awarded the bonus.

The LIKE Operator

The LIKE operator introduces us to wildcards. A wildcard character is an operator that does not select any one type of character but shifts depending on the character to be found. For example, if we looked into Store 1's account and wanted to select only last names that start with M. We have two options for wildcard operators: (%), which can select one or more characters, and (_), which only selects one.

```
SELECT lname from MemberDetails
WHERE lname LIKE 'M%';
```

The wildcard (%) would select only members whose last names begin with M. We use the LIKE operator to use wildcards. Wildcards do not require specific locations, and it is common to use more than one in a subquery.

Any use of the WHERE, INTO, HAVING, and FROM clauses condenses the amount of data to sift through exponentially. These *filtering conditions* can group and summarize data, as we've seen earlier in the chapter. The GROUP BY clause puts information into tidy columns, which can prevent duplication of data. Aggregation shows the summary of data entered, and the COUNT ( ) clause provides quick information into the number of data points in one or multiple tables. All of these filtering conditions make it easier for multiple people to access different data at the same time.

Summary

Grouping data, which becomes more useful in the chapters to come, refers to the selection of data inside a table. The queries associated with grouping may include the grouping of rows or columns, each designed to give a personalized view of the data. The HAVING clause is a subsection of grouping, essentially defining which data should appear in the grouped search. When searching for and grouping data, the NULL response may be present, which causes two tables to form: those with data associated with the query and those either without or of unknown value. Aggregation of data, or data summary, is done effectively through grouping by using the command COUNT ( ).

Filtering data is necessary for queries that hold a lot of data. Instead of spending hours delving into data tables and endless rows, filtering data puts the correct information in the right table, making seeing the information that much easier. Parentheses, the NOT operator, and the LIKE operator all specify which information should be displayed in a grouped table.

Chapter 6: Joins

Throughout this book, we have expressed the need for separating data into tables and decluttering information in your database. Though it may seem easier to search for data within a single table, it is not required. The JOIN command takes information from two tables to produce a single result. Queries from a single table are not uncommon, but you will often need information from two or more tables to get definitive answers.

Joins and Two-Table Queries

There are many reasons why we would use joins to gather data. Consider a business with information on employees and those of customers held in two different tables. Suppose we are looking for the name of an employee with the same last name as a customer to give the customer a family discount. Instead of using two queries to find the last name of the employee and then another to wade through the list of customers, a join command can provide a single answer from the two tables.

Now let's look at an example. Looking at a single customer, we want to know the name and credit limit of the person who placed the order. We have two different tables to consider:

Orders and Customers. Each has the name of the customer linked to the table, but the Customers table does not contain orders, and the orders table does not contain specific customer information like credit limit. Let's think through this logically, like we would with a pen and paper.

First, we need to find the names of the columns that hold the information. Both the Orders and Customers tables hold the customer ID, which links the results together. Next, find the order number and the amount charged at the time of sale. We'll connect this information with the first line of the query. We'll find the customer's data by finding the order number and connecting it with the credit limit and paste the information into the query results. (Groff & Weinberg, 2010). This is essentially what your database does when connecting two queries together from two separate tables.

Simple Joins

Joining tables is the process of taking two distinct tables and *joining* them together to create a new table. The process is also known as an *equi-join,* symbolizing that the exact columns from each table are transported to the new conjoined table. We've covered subqueries, grouping, and aggregation, and all these methods lead up to taking multiple queries with many groups of tables. To begin, however, we'll focus on simple joins that only involve the combination of two tables for one resulting table.

The relational database is built on the concept of tables communicating with one another. Information regarding the setup of a business is broken down into bite-sized parts that all connect with one another. For example, a dealership may have multiple employees listed in a table. Individual employees may have their own tables that contain their sales. Their sales are broken down into elements of their purchases, such as how much credit is attached to their purchase and what orders they received. That information may be broken down further to include individual payments per purchase. Though this is a broad example, it illustrates how many tables may be associated with a single piece of data, like a customer ID number. Joins utilize the relationships in a relational database to give unique tables that combine table subjects, and joins are the only way to relate the data across tables.

The common SELECT command comes in no less useful for joins. The SELECT statement accesses multiple tables at once, finding a condition that matches the query. The example query connects multiple tables.

SELECT CustomerID, Amount, Store

FROM StoreID, Orders

WHERE Customer = CustomerID

Like the queries from previous chapters, we select multiple data points, but this time the FROM statement contains two locations, StoreID and Orders. The WHERE clause uses the equality sign for comparison, using customer data from both tables. Notice that SQL did not specify how the task should be completed; the system infers what results you expect by looking at the FROM and WHERE clauses.

Parent/Child Queries

We briefly touched on parent/child queries in the previous chapters, but we'll discuss them more in detail here. Just as there is order to which table is subject to another, so is a child subject to a parent query. Let us take, for instance, the example of the store given previously. Each table associated with the company embodies smaller divisions that are associated with one another. To use our example above, an employee may belong to a large list of employees for a given store, but his or her customers belong in a table reserved for the sales made by that employee. Thus, the child (a customer to whom the employee has sold a product) is relevant to the parent (the employee who did the selling) in relation.

To utilize a parent/child join, we compare using primary and foreign keys. The primary keys are related to foreign keys through column comparison. A query for a parent/child relationship will include the location for both the child and the parent in the query. The query is expressed as a single table query, but the information is pulled from both locations.

SELECT Name, City

    FROM Salesperson, Offices

    WHERE SalesOffice = Office

The query pulls information from both the SalesPerson and Offices tables. The primary key that contains the original column in this example is the SalesOffice, and Office refers to the foreign key, the column that was added to break down the Salesperson table. The WHERE clause stipulates which columns will be accessed, and the SELECT command creates the information that will be added to the newly joined table.

Inner Joins

Similar to the parent/child queries, inner joins search for data matches in each table. Both inner joins and parent/child joins are represented in literature, and you'll likely see both of them listed in popular books. As the most widely used join, inner joins work with data from two different tables and create results matching data. The ON clause specifies which information will be joined. For example, we can create a table that contains data on both employees and administrators by using the JOIN and ON clauses.

SELECT Name, City, Title

```
FROM Employee JOIN Department

ON EmployeeID = DepartmentID
```

We are comparing both the employee and department IDs and joining them into another comprehensive table that includes both employees and every department. Instead of creating a long list of data that contains 500 rows, the ON clause causes the table to only include data that exists in both. For example, if the Employee table contains an employee ID for Karen with the value of 1, the department table with information about an entire department will only produce results if it contains one employee ID that is a match for Karen, or 1. This significantly cuts down the information listed in the table and makes searching much easier.

Inner joins do not disrupt the structure of existing databases. The table created from combining the two is a separate entity from the two that existed before. Information may be excluded when comparing the wrong tables, as is fairly obvious. Trying to find employees that work in a smaller department store that do not have the resources of a larger outlet may result in fewer department numbers. This is where being consistent in data entry is extremely valuable. For example, if a detailing division exists for dealership 1 but doesn't for dealership 2, department numbers may collide. A database cannot join information from two tables about departments that do not coincide with both dealerships.

Inner Joins: Equijoins and Non-Equijoins

Simple inner joins may be the most common types of joins, but there are times when gathering information from two different tables that match some data in the columns doesn't create a table that gives you all the data you need. More complex joins, such as cross-joins and self-joins, are required to fulfill tasks.

The difference between equijoins and non-equijoins is indicated in the names. Equijoins are the most common and involve equal signs. The equality signs provide comparisons directly from one column to another. Both tables do not require the same information. Most only require that the information is comparable at a basic level. The queries only require the same data type.

For example, let us say that Mary was hired on October 12, 2019. On the same day, there were twelve vehicle sales. The fact that Mary was hired on the same day that there were twelve sales have essentially nothing to do with one another, but we can still enter a query looking for more information about that day.

```
SELECT Vehicle_VIN, Saledate, Amount, Name
       FROM Salespeople, Vehicle_Sales
       WHERE Sale_Date = Hire_Date
```

SQL effectively creates a table that expresses the sale date of vehicles on October 12, 2019 and records who was hired on that day. Though this might not seem like the most practical way to create a table or have data displayed, it does give us a key insight into how SQL handles join queries.

Non-equijoins still provide a comparison test, but the data for non-equijoins involves inequalities. We've briefly expressed the importance of inequality functions, but we'll go into more depth here. The equality (=) provides a direct comparison, but queries that look for information regarding changes in averages or improvements are best expressed through inequalities such as (<) or (>).

Suppose we are looking for the dealerships who have had more success than others. All dealerships have a quota to reach, but some perform better in high-population sites like New York City or Washington D.C. We may see how New York City's dealership did in the last month.

SELECT Name, City, Quota, Target

    FROM Store5

    WHERE Quota > Target

The information received shows how well Store5 did with sales, creating a result that displays both the quote, target, and their differences.

The same principles apply for joins. Suppose we are looking for a comparison of all of our dealerships. We still use the inequality to express the difference in the quota and target, but the information from which we receive the information will come from tables labeled Salespeople and Offices.

```
SELECT Name, Location, Quota, Target
    FROM Salespeople, Offices
    WHERE Quota > Target
```

The resulting table gives the sales numbers for the quota and target amounts listed by name, location, quota, and target amount. Non-equijoins are excellent comparison test, but they are not used as frequently as equijoins. Both, however, are important in data comparison from two or more tables.

Complex and Multiple Table Joins

When creating multiple joins, some query commands are altered. New syntax is required to execute multiple joins including filter conditions, qualified column names, all-column selections, self-joins, cross joins, and table aliases.

Qualified Column Names

Often when creating tables, multiple tables will contain the same column names. For example, a table marked Store1 may have the column name EmployeesID, and the table marked

Store2 may include the same information but for the second location. When executing a query with two tables that hold the same information, an error occurs.

SELECT Name, City, Sales

FROM Store1, Store2

WHERE Salespeople = Offices

ERROR: Ambiguous column name "Sales"

SQL cannot determine which column you are trying to access when you're looking for the column Sales. Because the store name and city may be different for each store, SQL can determine which location you are trying to access the information. However, since the sales are different for each store, SQL returns an ambiguous error.

This is where qualified column names come into play. To determine which information belongs to which table, we have to separate the column names in the query to match the table in which they are located. A qualified column name includes both the table and column names separated by a period (Groff & Wienberg, 2010). To eliminate the ambiguity here, we will specify sales by naming the column names with both table and column information.

Store1.Sales

Store2.Sales

Instead of giving an invalid response, putting in the query with the specified column names will now give us the right results.

SELECT Name, City, Store1.Sales

FROM Store1, Store2

WHERE Salespeople = Offices

When creating queries for multiple tables, it becomes essential to use this method to send queries through SQL. Multiple tables will no doubt include generic column names such as CustomerID, EmployeeID, and Sales. The only drawback to this method is the resulting length of the queries, which become considerably longer.

All-Column Selections

As we've discussed in the past, the SELECT command will be one of the most useful commands in all of SQL. When it comes to multiple table queries, it becomes the tool you use for both column and table names. The SELECT * command selects all information in a given table. If you continue the query by using FROM and selecting multiple tables and WHERE to indicate which columns, SQL will create a table that all column data for both tables. For instance, suppose we want to view the columns associated with Store1 and Store2 that show employees for both companies and where they work.

SELECT *

> FROM Store1, Store2
>
> WHERE SalesOffice = Office

All information from Store1 regarding salespeople will show in the table first, then Store2's information will follow.

Though we are discussing this in the multiple joins sections, use common sense when using this command. The example just given includes information from a large table, and specified tables will give you more relevant data. Also, when combining two or more tables, the data received can become overwhelming. Keep in mind that you may not want to exhibit a table that contains large numbers of rows.

Table Aliases

Table aliases cut down on unnecessarily long queries and are vital in self-joins. When referencing a table outside using the FROM clause, you have two options: use the entire name of the table or use an alias (Beaulieu, 2009). Table aliases are shortened versions of the table names. For example, when using the FROM clause, we can avoid long queries and connect the names of tables necessary in the query.

> FROM Salespeople.Name

becomes

> FROM S.Name

Columns, too, follow this rule. To shorten the name of a column, define it through the AS command.

SELECT Employees AS E

Self-Joins

Self-joins essentially tie a table to itself. Why would you do this? Finding duplicate information is one of the reasons you may consider this crazy type of join. Another reason may be that there is a relationship with data inside your table. Consider, for example, that you want to find employee IDs and their managers. You do not want a list that contains only employees and manager because there is no definitive relationship listed unless you want to wade through columns of data to find it. We would create this self-join by using employee IDs as our primary keys. Managers within the table are linked to the employee IDs, so the Managers column is actually an example of a foreign key. The relationship between manager and employee is found through our comparison test.

So, if we give the SELECT command to find names within the table, it should find all of the names and listed them one by one, right?

SELECT Name, name

This would result in an error. When entering the SELECT command, we are instructing SQL to find all names within a table. If we ask SQL to give us two columns with names, the table assumes you want two columns with the same names listed on each one. This type of query is not permitted. We have to specify that we want to select the names of the employees and managers, which both have employee IDs, so we will use our qualified table name to select EmployeeID.Name and Managers.Name instead.

When we're entering a query for a self-join, it would make sense to create a query that would select only from that table. So, it would make sense that the queries should only specify that table.

FROM Employee_File, Employee_File

FROM Employee_File

The first confuses an SQL system because it does not differentiate from where the data comes. The first option is illegal because of its duplication. The second command listed looks like a single file query. If we select that option for our FROM clause, we will receive a data list identical to the list of all employees. This will not show relationships between the two types of employees. The command, therefore, must include the files for employees and managers, discovering the relationships between the two.

For the WHERE clause, we might expect to write down a command that compared the two lists: employees and managers.

> WHERE EmployeeID = Managers

While this may work when looking in multiple tables, the results yield an error since managers are still employees. We cannot duplicate the entries. The solution, therefore, is to once again separate the columns with qualified column names, eventually giving us the right query.

> SELECT EmployeeID.Name, Managers.Name
>
> FROM EmployeeID, Managers
>
> WHERE EmployeeID.Managers = Managers.EmployeeID

The comparison test allows us to see the relationship between the employee and manager, and a table is created to follow that design. The format of the names follows *table aliases*, which differentiate columns within the table. To create aliases, use the command AS to define certain columns within the table.

Cross Joins

To understand cross joins, let us first go back to the basic mathematics of an SQL database. Arithmetic, such as multiplication, can connect two tables together, just as you might see in mathematics. Also called the Cartesian, the multiplication of the two tables produced another called the *product table*. Multiplication, often symbolized by a cross sign, provides the name for the CROSS JOIN command.

Because there are no to very few columns just marked with numbers, it is illogical to assume that the multiplication between two tables would yield combined results of the columns. Instead, the product table arranges itself with the first table mentioned in the command followed by the second table.

Just as we have always done in the past, a cross join starts with the SELECT command. The FROM clause holds the CROSS JOIN command which multiplies the two tables that were selected together.

SELECT Employees.Name, Customer.Name, City

FROM Store1.Sales CROSS JOIN Store2.Sales

Another way to enter this data is to simply leave out the CROSS JOIN command and separate the FROM statements by a comma.

SELECT Employees.Name, Customer.Name, City

FROM Store1.Sales, Store2.Sales

With the exclusion of the WHERE statement and the use of the CROSS JOIN command, SQL combines the two tables' columns into one.

Outer Joins

Most of the joins that we have discussed have pertained to inner joins, which, granted, is the most common type of join you will see. However, outer joins do not require matching columns to create a relationship. Outer joins look for related rows for pairing and combine them to create new tables. Many databases require the name of the table and column, but this is not always the case: "While this is true of GROUP BY and WHERE clauses, it's not strictly necessary in the column selection part of the SELECT statement unless it's not clear which table the column is from, such as when two or more tables have columns with the same name" (Colby & Wilton, 2005).

As we have discussed joins involve the connection of two tables. What happens, though, when we want to find accounts that are specialized and link those two tables together? Two accounts that have similar data will return with a table that marries the columns from the tables that are joined. If we create a table that shows the accounts of customers 1 through 10, we will receive a table that shows the accounts corresponding to each customer ID. If those customers had more than one account, then they will be listed more than once.

Suppose, however, that the table marking the customer IDs only accepts business IDs in our join with their accounts. In an inner join, the only accounts that would show are those linked to business names, significantly cutting down the list.

Suppose that there are only three business accounts in the 1 to 10 business IDs we look for in our query. If the businesses each have two accounts, we will receive six rows. The successful inner join only shows us the information for business accounts.

What if, however, we want to see all accounts listed but only specify the names of the business accounts? The OUTER JOIN command then shows us a table with all customer accounts and IDs with the NULL response for customer IDs that are not business accounts. When querying in SQL, an unknown value receives a NULL response. NULL returned values express the lack of data in that area. However, during an outer join, we are intentionally leaving that information out, resulting in the NULL response.

Let us look at another example. Say, for instance, we want to see a list of girls and boys from two different schools. The Elementary School table shows information for the children Rachel, Joseph, Link, Dan, Elizabeth, and Mary. We also want to find the list of children in Middle School, so the table we create will show a pairing of the children there: Juan, Lisa, Todd, Susan. Some, however, went to completely different elementary and middle school, which we will name Elementary1 School and Middle1 School. We want to join the two tables to see all of the results of kids in both Elementary School and Middle School. We are looking for pairs of boys and girls that went to the same schools and list them according to the school he or she attended. Table 6.1 shows the resulting table.

Girls.Name	Girls.School	Boys.Name	Boys.School
Rachel	Elementary School	Joseph	Elementary School
Elizabeth	Elementary School	Link	Elementary School
Mary	Elementary School	Dan	Elementary School
Lisa	Middle School	Juan	Middle School
Susan	Middle School	Todd	Middle School
Penelope	Elementary1 School	NULL	NULL
Heather	NULL	NULL	NULL

NULL	NULL	Russ	Middle1 School
NULL	NULL	Josh	NULL

Table 6.1: Outer Join

Penelope and Russ each have no pair on the table, so the results for their partners are left as NULL. Heather and Josh have no information regarding school. This could be due to homeschooling or transfers, so the rest of their rows show NULL.

It is possible that either girl or boy names could appear twice in each name column. We are looking for matching information, so, if there is one more girl than boy associated with Elementary School, it's possible that there could be multiple entries for one child. This is called *information preserving*, and SQL uses it to keep like paired records together.

Left Outer Joins

The outer join we just completed is an example of a full join. Full joins allow for both sides of the resulting table to have NULL values. Left outer joins, however, restrict information to the left side to only allow data from the first table to show non-NULL values. In our example above, only the girls' data would be in a resultant table subject to a left outer join.

Think about what we might call the *dominant* table. In a full join, both tables displayed all information assigned to both tables. The dominant table for an outer join is the first table listed. So, in our last example, the Girls table is listed first, so for a left outer join, we define the outer join in the next code.

```
SELECT *
        FROM Girls, Boys
            WHERE Girls.School LEFT OUTER JOIN Boys.School
```

As a side note, you'll notice that the left and right outer joins have a slightly different syntax than the full outer join we mentioned earlier. Both are correct, but the language is slightly more concise in the full outer join. We'll use the same syntax here.

```
SELECT *
        FROM Girls, Boys
            WHERE Girls.School *= Boys.School
```

The asterisk before the equivalence sign defines our requirement for a left outer join while the asterisks before and after the equivalence signs define a full outer join. The same can be worked for a right outer join with the asterisk located on the right side of the equal sign. But let us return to the left outer join.

The queries listed above result in a table like the one listed in Table 6.2.

Girls.Name	Girls.School	Boys.Name	Boys.School
Rachel	Elementary School	Joseph	Elementary School
Elizabeth	Elementary School	Link	Elementary School
Mary	Elementary School	Dan	Elementary School
Lisa	Middle School	Juan	Middle School
Susan	Middle School	Todd	Middle School

| Penelope | Elementary 1 School | NULL | NULL |
| Heather | NULL | NULL | NULL |

Table 6.2: The left outer join.

Again, all information from the Girls table is mentioned on the left, including the NULL value in the last entry. However, in our initial table, the last two entries did not have any values listed in the Girls.Name or Girls.School columns, so the rest of the Boys' information is taken from the resulting table. Because there is no data in the Girl's column for the last two rows, SQL only takes into account the filled data points and ignores unreceived information.

All data listed in a table is monitored by the database, and if there are multiple entries for columns on the left side, they will be divided into individual points on the right. For example, if we are reviewing two film genre tables, we may receive more than one entry for the Horror section. Suppose that our data on the right consists of films dedicated to the genre. It's common to see more than one entry. If this is the case, SQL divides the entries into sections on the right side, still including all data points.

Right Outer Join

The right outer join is the opposite of the left outer join, so we'll move through this section quickly. A right outer join accepts all information for a result table for the right side of the FROM clause. As such, the dominant table listed in the query is on the right side of the equality.

SELECT *

   FROM Girls, Boys

   WHERE   Girls.School   RIGHT   OUTER   JOIN Boys.School

Once again, there are two forms to this query, but the first is wordy, so the syntax for the second is preferred. Both, however, give the same information, so you can choose either one.

SELECT *

   FROM Girls, Boys

   WHERE Girls.School =* Boys.School

Our updated table favors the Boys table now, and Table 6.3 illustrates the results.

Girls.Name	Girls.School	Boy.Name	Boys.School
Rachel	Elementary	Joseph	Elementary

	School		School
Elizabeth	Elementary School	Link	Elementary School
Mary	Elementary School	Dan	Elementary School
Lisa	Middle School	Juan	Middle School
Susan	Middle School	Todd	Middle School
NULL	NULL	Russ	Middle1 School
NULL	NULL	Josh	NULL

Table 6.2: Right outer join

Union Joins

At times, it is necessary to combine queries that have seemingly no connection. It's not uncommon to want to see information seemingly unrelated but has a correlation with your notes. We've briefly gone over cross joins and outer joins, and union joins share many of the same characteristics. We are essentially combining two tables together, regardless of primary keys, foreign keys, or similar data.

One of the rules for a union join is that the first table must contain the same number of columns as the second table. The union join connects the two tables into the same number of columns because the data is displayed together. The union join differs from the cross join due to its combination of columns. The cross join combines already-existing tables, effectively adding the columns from one table to the other. The union join, however, creates a table with only the specified number of columns with the same data types.

If you're wondering what data types are, don't worry. It's easier to define than you think. Consider a query combining two tables and their columns together.

```
SELECT        Dealership_name,        Dealership_phone,
Dealership_city

      FROM Company

      UNION

SELECT Film_genre, Film_rating, Film_name

      FROM Film_Categories
```

Though the two tables and columns seem completely unrelated, the UNION command forces these two tables to create a resulting table that includes both types of data. Notice that the data types we are matching have something in common: the first and third columns have alphabet characters, and the second column contains only numeric data. It is this style of data types that allow us to combine the two. The resulting table will have both dealership names and film genres in the first column, the second column will contain numeric data in the form of phone numbers and film ratings, and the final column will show dealership cities and the names of films. This is rather a random selection of combined tables, but SQL will still combine all files to give you a comprehensive table of each column combined.

When executing a query with the UNION command and only accessing numeric files, you may see strange results. For example, let us assume that we have two tables: Dealerships and Films. If we combine the two in a union query using only their IDs, we will receive a table that only has a list of numbers listed in ascending order. If there are duplicate IDs, they won't show in the list as SQL automatically filters out all duplicates, giving a refined table that may not be as helpful.

However, using the UNION ALL clause, SQL will reveal a table that has all data in the file, regardless of duplicates.

SELECT DealershipID

   FROM Dealerships

   UNION ALL

```
SELECT FilmID

    FROM Films
```

Variations to display the table information are easily made through clauses such as ORDER BY and GROUP BY.

The SELECT and UNION commands display information in an opposite way from each other. If we wanted to select data from a dealership and there were multiple accounts linked to each employee ID, the duplicate rows would show in a query specific to the employee ID. It is only the SELECT DISTINCT command that would prevent duplicate entries. The UNION operator, however, follows the opposite principle. When selecting an employee's ID that is tied with multiple customer accounts, SQL automatically deletes the duplicated information. If we want to include all IDs regardless of duplication, the UNION ALL must be included in the query.

Like mentioned previously, knowing data type is essential to creating unions. Data types are created through the creation of the database, so it may be difficult to decipher which columns contain numeric or character data. For instance, the film ID in an SQL query may appear to be a number, but if the creator of the database used the ID with a character variant, such as defining each ID by a shortened version of the name, the query would be impossible to create. Determine what data type exists for each column through single table queries if you plan on creating unions between two tables.

Summary

Joins are processes that allow data from two tables or, in the case of self-joins, one table, create relationships with each other through primary keys, foreign keys, and parent/child relationships.

Inner joins that connect data through relationships are the most common types of joins, and it is likely most of your queries will involve them in one way or another. We can compare joins through equalities or inequalities, called equijoins and non-equijoins, respectively. The comparison of two tables and/or columns are done through these tests.

Complex and multiple table joins require rules in order to complete successfully. Qualified column names must include no repeated names and those that are unique in their table locations. All-column selections provide data specific to a column with all rows included. It is often necessary to view all data points from two tables with like information to determine differences. Table aliases make comparisons easier and specify which table should how which data.

Self-joins are joins within the same table. These may be used to compare data from one section to another or to order data based on one column's comparison with another. Cross joins, similar to multiplied tables, takes the data from one table and tacks on the columns from another to create a new table.

Outer joins include data that may show as NULL in an inner join. The NULL values indicate that there is no information present or the information does not meet the standards of the database. Left and right joins use the full outer join principles but with only certain sides showing the NULL data. Union joins connect two tables and columns with information from any part of the database, regardless of connection.

Chapter 7: Views

Coding for a marketer may seem like a stretch, but people from all departments in a business need access to a database to make the company grow. Views give other people working with the database the ability to see certain aspects of the database without having to input large amounts of code. Views are gateways to tables containing real information that make it easier to see what tables contain.

What Are Views?

Just as we explained before, views are ways others can view information without having to enter long lines of code. But what are they exactly? Views are virtual tables that hold no actual information, but they are linked to tables that do. Views are highly personalized. Each department in a company can have different views in which to see data. The marketing team, for instance, may have a different view than the sales team. Information in marketing, such as statistics gained from social media exposure, are not necessary for the sales team, who may need to know the added costs to a vehicle.

Views also bring security to a database. Views can restrict which information is shown in a database through monitoring the columns and rows exhibited. For example, a salesperson may need to know the birthday, phone number, and VIN for a car they sell, but only managers can see the social security number of each customer. The program allows for selective shown information, which, through specialized views for large companies, can break down information to only show to people in certain departments, thus creating a secure database.

A view appears to be a real table with full access to all columns and rows, but we can pick and choose which information is shown in each view. Data is only available through query results, and the information added to a database only appears to tie to the table. You might say that views are the bodyguards of your SQL database: data coming in goes through the bodyguard and straight to the manager, but the public only gets to see some of the information once entered.

Views, though highly useful, also have limitations. During the creation of views, a query is saved in the system for future use. Essentially, views are queries saved under query names (Colby & Wilton, 2005). During normal business processes, views may add upon each other until long lines of only views separate the query from the data, creating processing issues and seriously slowing down production. This same structure of adding views upon each other also interferes with updates to tables. Since the information is going through long lines of queries, it may take some time before data can reach its initial table. Views are put in place to simplify lives. That means that if there are too many views clogging up the pathway to the initial table, the inputted views have not been properly utilized.

Creating Views

When creating views, the first step is to select the data for entry. Single tables or joins can be formatted into views, and are created through the SELECT command. Starting a view with one table allows users to piece together the information already locked inside the table and view it more easily. The CREATE VIEW command begins the process.

CREATE VIEW Customer_Processing

SELECT Name, Address, Phone_number, Car_sale

　　　　FROM Customer_Filing

Now any time we want to look at the view, all we need to do is send a query to view it.

SELECT *

　　　　FROM Customer_Processing

It is important to keep in mind that the SQL language changes slightly with every platform. In our example above, we used the SELECT * command to select all data from the view we created. Another command that is similar is SELECT ALL. Be aware of which syntax your platform suggests using. It will become essential when creating views and manipulating data.

RDMSs use views to create connections between a query and the database. If the query is simple enough, it will create a view at that moment, piecing together data row by row. Larger and more sophisticated tables, however, take more time to complete. To save you time, RDMSs save tables for future use. Once the view is created, you can access it at any time and the RDMS displays the saved table.

Types of Views

All views have a base. Consider, for example, that you want to analyze how many people are in attendance at a conference. The information that you pull would contain data like name, days attended, workshops attended, and comments for improvement. This list is very small, and it is intended to be. We are simply looking for the raw data associated with the basics of the conference. As such, we create views associated with this data. In the future, if data is changed or added, we modify the view to suit our needs.

Table Join Views

The simplest of views in the table join views. If we are looking for information regarding two sets of data, like an individual employee's sales and a customer list, we create a join that condenses the information into one table. Like our discussion of joins before, the view created will combine data through an SQL query and display it in the view. Table join views are also known as base queries, which essentially means that they are the simplest kinds of queries and are easy to manipulate.

Horizontal Views

Horizontal views provide limited access to a table. For example, if two software development companies were located on opposite sides of the US, it would be unnecessary for them to view sales information in the same table as the other. After all, that information does not pertain to them. Horizontal views could determine which data is viewed by both sides, giving a customized view.

```
CREATE VIEW EASTCOAST_REPS AS
SELECT *
      FROM Salesreps
      WHERE Salesreps_Office IN (1, 3, 13, 14, 15)
```

Likewise, we can create a view for the west coast sales reps.

```
CREATE VIEW WESTCOAST_REPS AS
SELECT *
      FROM Salesreps
      WHERE Salesreps_Office IN (2, 4, 5, 10, 11, 12)
```

Though the term "denying access" seems rather harsh, it is intended to provide customized views with only information specific to one section of the company. The customized views can pertain to any section of the company as well, dividing the data into sections that only some parts of the company need.

Horizontal queries also allow joined queries. For instance, if a company looks for employees and customers on the west coast, we can use a join and horizontal query.

```
CREATE VIEW CUSTOMERS&EMPLOYEES_WESTCOAST
AS
SELECT *
    FROM CustomerID, EmployeeID
    WHERE Customers = Employees IN (1, 2, 3, 6, 12)
```

This query allows us to use two different techniques to create a table that shows us both customers and employees for the west coast store. The additional horizontal view query breaks down the information further, allowing the company on the west coast to only see certain information. This happens frequently, as it is often important to see multiple sets of data at once.

Vertical Views

Like horizontal views, vertical views only show specified columns in a table. The vertical view is an excellent way to secure a database. For example, if a company that sells used vehicles collects sensitive information, such as birth date and social security number, a SQL RDMS can restrict which columns are necessary for receptionists to see. Since the receptionist may need to take payments and handle credit cards, he or she would need access to payment information, but social security numbers and birth dates are excluded from her view.

A vertical view would also be common when decluttering information seen by different employees at the dealership. When a car is sold, information about the car's make, model, VIN, color, etc., are linked to the customer's information. The table for the sold car, therefore, may be part of a join that connects the customer's information with the car sold. All data on both the customer and vehicle create a long line of columns in a joined table, most of which is not necessary to view unless needed. Therefore, a query may specify only certain columns to make accessing the information faster and more efficient.

CREATE VIEW JOHN_DAVIS_VEHICLE

SELECT Name, Type_of_sale, Date_sold, Amount_due, Make, Model, VIN, Year

    FROM John_Davis, MazdaRX8

    WHERE John_Davis = MazdaRX8

The receptionist taking the payment of Mr. John Davis needs only to see this information to take a credit card payment. The rest of the data about the car, including photos and general information, and John Davis, which may include a co-buyer or favorite racetrack, is completely unnecessary to complete a transaction. Producing this view, therefore, requires far less time to create, speeding up processing time.

Field Views

Field views are those in which only certain information is shown. This simplified view shows all fields requested in the query. Field views essentially take the information from the table and display it as it would for a table created in an SQL system.

Row/Column Subset Views

It may become inconvenient to create only horizontal and vertical views that show all columns and rows respectively. The SQL language allows for the condensed version of both columns and rows. Its command is simple, just like those listed above, but it reflects only specific columns and rows. We are creating a view related to Eleanor, our customer service representative, whose ID number is 22. We want to see all information regarding her clients.

```
CREATE VIEW ELEANOR AS
```

```
SELECT CustomerID, Company

    FROM Customers

    WHERE Employee = 22
```

We are able to see every customer that Eleanor has and only the customer ID and company for which they work.

Grouped Views

Grouped views are very similar to grouped queries, where every group is definitively selected by the GROUP BY clause. Grouped views summarize data and place the data into one row per section, creating rows by the grouped amounts (Groff & Weinberg, 2010). Grouped views, however, use the data found through the group query and put it into a virtual table accessed through a view query. For example, a manager wants to see which sales were made by each salesperson, and he or she is interested in the averages over the course of their times working at the establishment. The manager wants to group salespeople.

```
CREATE VIEW SALES_AVE (Who, High, Low, Avg, Total) AS

SELECT SalesID, Count (*), MIN (AMOUNT), MAX
(AMOUNT), AVG (AMOUNT)

    FROM West_coast_sales

    GROUP BY Salesperson
```

The manager, in this case, is able to see how many sales were made, the minimum, maximum, and the average. Instead of large chunks of data piled into columns randomly, the SQL database groups each salesperson into his or her own row. The view, in turn, becomes more readable.

Because grouped views provide a summary of all information listed in the rows, the SQL processor must work overtime to produce all data. The RDMS takes a lot of time to process the data, which means the view takes a substantial amount of processing to maintain a grouped view (Groff & Weinberg, 2010).

In the example above, the summary of each salesperson includes the minimum, maximum, total, and average of all sales made. The view above cannot be maintained, and it should be clear why. Because views access information from a real table, they are subject to change. However, grouped views provide only a snapshot of the information included in the tables. Grouped tables provide a *group* of information of rows together. If we decided to send a request through an SQL query to update the information, the RDMS would not be able to comply. Columns in a group are connected to each other and, therefore, do not correspond to any particular column in any table, making updating the information impossible.

Joined Views

Joined views, similar to grouped views, take up a lot of RDMS processing time. The processing of combining a virtual table to show information from two or more tables takes considerable time. However, creating the view is possible and easily retrievable once it has been created. Consider a franchise that has only recently grown. The CEO started the company years ago and still likes to see things the old fashion way. He or she wants to see his employees listed by name instead of a number. The CEO is looking for a table that shows each customer listed by name, order amount, and type of sale. The view developed for the CEO would contain multiple joins due to the wide array of data requested.

CREATE VIEW EMPLOYEE_RECORD (Customer_name, Order_amount, Type_of_sale, Employee_name)

SELECT Customer_name, Order_amount, Type_of_sale, Employee_name

FROM Orders, Employees

WHERE Employee_name = EmployeeID

The CEO would see a view that consisted of customer name, order amount, type of sale, and employee name. Since the table is listed with employee IDs to make listing easier, the WHERE statement expresses that the employee name must be included as a substitute for the employee ID.

Joined views, once created, make processing information from a real table easier to manage. With the view created, the only requirement to access the data is to process a single-table query. The view provides easier access to information without joining two or more tables.

Updating Views

When more than one person is accessing a view, there may come a time when multiple people may need to update the view at the same time. Multiple people accessing a view and updating the data is not done through direct access to the table though. Views can be updated on the grounds of a few rules as defined by Beauleu.

- The view must not include any summary clauses such as MIN ( ), MAX ( ), AVG ( ), etc.

- The view must not include any HAVING or GROUP BY clauses.

- The view must not include subqueries in the SELECT or FROM clauses, and the WHERE clause must not include any tables referenced in the FROM clause.

- The view must not include UNION, UNION ALL, or DISTINCT.

- The FROM clause must include at least one table or updatable view.

- The FROM clause must only use joins if there is more than one table or review (2009).

Updatable views are necessary to maintain current information. For example, in our horizontal view above, we mentioned that only some of the rows would be visible to the west and east coast departments. What if, however, one of the accounts requires an addendum added to its account. Inserting, deleting, and updating views should be possible without forcing the view to be created again.

Checking Updates

When updating a view, it is common to think that the INSERT and UPDATE commands will result in an updated system. However, if inserting or updating rows in the database do not agree with RDMS standards, the view will not change. Updatable views must follow the rules above but so must the changes to views. However, SQL allows for a checking option to prevent others from adding queries that are unable to pass inspection.

Since many views are created on top of one another, many contain checks that follow the hierarchy of the views down to the table with the real data. The view, therefore, must include WITH CASCADED CHECK OPTION when checking every view built on top of one another. SQL automatically chooses the cascaded version of checking whenever the CHECK OPTION is listed without a specification.

Views that are checked locally, however, are slightly faster and easier to process. Just as with the CHECK OPTION command for the cascaded check, a local check is also possible. The WITH LOCAL CHECK OPTION command only checks the current view and does not reach further down the line.

Checks prevent viewers of the program to modify data that is not in their control. Building in a check keeps accidental data from creating data corruption and errors within the system.

Dropping Views

Just like dropping tables, dropping views is sometimes necessary in order to keep up with constantly changing data. Dropping a view uses the DROP VIEW command, and it is easily implemented after a view is created. Imagine, for example, that the view we created concerning viewing employee records has come to a standstill. The information listed in that view is no longer up to date, and it is time to delete the data to prevent further confusion. As the table has already been named, we use that same name and the command DROP VIEW to delete the table.

DROP VIEW EMPLOYEE_RECORD

The data regarding the view disappears. Luckily, the table that held the data for the view is still intact. Any changes to it in the future can be used to create additional views.

Grouped views are also common to delete. Since they only include data that are a snapshot of information at one point in time, it is common to delete grouped views to clear up space in the database.

Materialized Views

As we have mentioned before, if views are created simply (like single-table views, row/column subsets, or field views), creating a view is easy, and the RDMS works quickly through the view to create a virtual table on the spot. These views require little processing, which makes them highly accessible. The RDMS uses the simplest path to completion in creating views from simple queries. Updating, inserting, and deleting data is easy through these types of views. SQL simply sends the query directly from the view into the database, serving as a proverbial middle-man to the operation. As long as the view query follows the same rules as those listed above, the query makes changes to the original table.

However, if a view is created from complex tables and queries (like multiple joins or unions), creating the pathway directly from the view to the table becomes far more difficult, and it often requires extreme processing capabilities. To combat some of the processing time results, the RDMS sometimes creates a temporary table that completes the query from the view and changes the information from the original table through the temporary table until the query is finished. This complex system also causes large processing times and less efficiency in the database.

Materialized views are the solution that the RDMS develops to combat the slow processing speed and loss of efficiency. If the query is complex, the RDMS creates a view that has become a table that accepts queries such as updates, inserts, and deletions. The non-materialized views, in turn, are those views that only hold the virtual data. Though a materialized view sounds like the most efficient way to send a query through a complex view, there is a trade-off in efficiency versus processing speed. Non-materialized views are more efficient since they send data directly to the database. The time to create a connection between the view and table requires a lot of processing, but it is slightly more efficient. Materialized views, on the other hand, run as though sending data straight to a table and do not lose prospective time. The process in which it takes the view to create a temporary table and save it, however, is less efficient.

Summary

Brandon Cooper

Views are individual sections of data that act as virtual tables for people across a database. People in accounting may see different views from those on a sales team. Views are created through using the CREATE VIEW command, which requires that all data requested be placed in a virtual table with full access to others in the system. Join views, horizontal views, and vertical views subset the data into data only applicable to some people within a database. Horizontal views take only the rows necessary, and vertical views take on the columns necessary for viewing in a database. This provides customized views for different departments in a company. Field views, row/column subset views, grouped views, and joined views also serve the same purpose with each query that creates these views condensing information into tables that are accessible and relevant to departments.

Views are updated only through a subset of rules that define if the view can, in fact, be updated. Views that create queries and create temporary tables that complete the view provide more efficiency within a database but lack the same processing time. Dropping views are easy through the DROP VIEW command, deleting the virtual table.

Chapter8:Managing Transaction Processing

SQL databases are practical for many reasons. Though we have explored ways to show the data acquired, SQL offers much more to everyday businesses. Transaction processing is more than processing a credit card. A transaction involves several steps, all of which are recorded in an SQL sequence.

For example, if an order is processed for a department store, the database must make several changes:

1. The order must be processed.

2. The transaction completed must enter data about the customer and card information.

3. The customer and sale information must be included in the salesperson's file.

4. The sale must be recorded in the store's order table.

5. The product table must update the number of the product at the store's site.

These are just a few considerations for processing transactions. The information included in every sale affects the tables around it, and information is constantly added and updated in the database.

What is a Transaction?

A transaction is defined in the SQL language as a group of statements pulled together to form a logical unit of work (Groff & Weinberg, 2010). Transactions work together through actions dependent upon each other, as was illustrated above. Any change to a transaction must include the changing or altering of data associated.

Transactions must depend upon one another. This means that if one action is made, the others must follow suit. It is like your right leg walking backward while your left leg and the rest of your body continues forward. The end result is either a bruised face or a twisted joint. But let us think about this from a business standpoint. Imagine you are paid to perform a magic act. The patrons who visit the theater must pay to enter the building, but they must also have an assigned seat. The transaction begins in an online shop to enter tickets. Their seats must be saved, so their data must be entered. Their names are put on file for emailed promotions. Essentially, the customer not only gets the show, but they must also receive the transactions that are a part of the experience.

Consistent data is essential to a transaction. If each of the cogs move separately from one another, the organization of the data collapses. Consider what a transaction with a hospital might mean. When records are entered for a patient, they also receive a room, bed, and procedure. Let us consider what this would mean for a surgery patient. If even one of these orders is not fulfilled, the organization falls apart. A patient may have the room, bed, and procedure, but if the records do not exist, the patient may receive a tonsillectomy instead of an appendectomy. If everything is provided except for a room, the patient could have to recover in the parking lot out back. Consistent logical statements produce effective transactions.

Each transaction should act as though there is a view of the end of the transaction. For instance, if a customer ordered a coffee at a cafe and changed his or her mind after the order was completed, the transaction should be effectively deleted instead of creating a second order that can only be completed at the end of the fulfillment of the coffee order. Each isolated transaction should be independent of other transactions to prevent unnecessary data pileup.

At the end of a transaction, the data must be saved appropriately. If a fire, lightning, or the apocalypse happens to come, it is important to have a location where all data is safely locked away. Losing internet connection may seem almost impossible in most cities, but if a database is not backed up properly and there is a temporary lapse in the connection a database can make with the internet, transactions cannot be completed successfully. Durability is extremely important in creating transactions.

Transaction Models

Most SQL databases are set up with similar ways to track the progress of a transaction. Again, since transactions are long groups of queries that are logically connected with one another, all queries must be completed for a successful transaction. Either all queries work to create a successful transaction, or if any of the processes fail, the transaction fails.

Transaction Types

The BEGIN TRANSACTION

The BEGIN TRANSACTION command starts a transaction. The SQL system starts the process to run through a transaction. The BEGIN TRANSACTION is also used for starting a process after another has completed.

The COMMIT TRANSACTION

The COMMIT TRANSACTION response determines that the transaction was completed successfully. A successful transaction displays the accuracy of the database's transaction process. This means that all steps to complete the transaction were successful. Once a transaction has received a COMMIT TRANSACTION response, it cannot be undone.

The SAVE TRANSACTION

Commonly, when a transaction is in progress, the SQL system will choose a point at which to save the process. The SAVE TRANSACTION command specifies these saving points for the future. When a rollback occurs, the automatic response from an SQL system is to roll the process back to the beginning of the transaction, but saving checkpoints in the process can save time and effort.

The ROLLBACK TRANSACTION

ROLLBACK TRANSACTION is a common term even outside of SQL. A rollback within the system, however, means that some part of the transaction has failed. It is not uncommon to see a list of procedures done correctly and simply stop when a process fails to complete a step. When updating a system or retrieving files linked to each other and an internet connection is lost, an error occurs and forces the progress to roll back, requiring internet access to complete the transaction.

Transaction Logs

Storing information about how a process works is one of the most important parts of creating a database. When setting up a transaction, the transaction logs keep the formula of the transaction for future use. Transactions performed on a database may be processed only one at a time, but what happens when large corporations start using a database and all processes are locked in? There could be dozens or hundreds of people working on the same database at the same time, which makes keeping track of all transaction processes essential.

A transaction log looks at a process before and after it completes and saves a model of it for future use. For example, if a company installs an update for their SQL software, the file created to complete the transaction must follow the guidelines given in the transaction log. Each step to run the update (such as implementing form revisions, editing tax information, or applying security measures for database access) is carefully documented just in case the process must be restarted.

Transaction logs are generally kept in a location separate to the other files in the system. If a power outage or unfortunate disaster happens to affect the way the transaction communicates with the database, keeping a transaction log can start the process from scratch or through saved points in the transaction procedure.

Not all SQL providers have transaction logs, and you should be aware of what type of provider works best for your needs. Transaction logs may cause some performance issues, and this is due to the extra space they require. As noted earlier, the process for creating and maintaining these transaction logs could mean extra work and slower processing times. If you are looking for a small database to begin, you may choose to find a provider that does not include transaction logs to improve efficiency. However, lack of transaction logs also puts you at risk of losing all data during a catastrophe.

Concurrent Transactions and Locking

It is inevitable that creating a database for a large company will yield constant access to the database. But what happens when there are multiple people accessing the SQL system and making changes on their own? SQL provides a basis to allow current transactions to work at the same time, and locking is one of the methods used to handle conflict between multiple entries.

Concurrent Transactions

SQL requires that, when working with two or more concurrent transactions, the database will appear as if no other transaction is taking place. This is because, if data is accessed and manipulated at the same time with resulting changes to the database, possible data corruption could occur. SQL takes care of this by limiting what is viewed on one section of the database and what is viewed on the other.

According to Groff and Weinberg's *Complete Reference to SQL,* transactions are set up to be independent of each other in an SQL system. Transactions are what keep the database from inputting data from outside locations that may cause data corruption. Transactions both copy and control data within a SQL system: "If two transactions, A and B, are executing concurrently, the DBMS ensures that the results will be the same as they would be if either (a) Transaction A were executed first, followed by Transaction B, or (b) Transaction B were executed first, followed by Transaction A" (2010). SQL effectively makes each user process transactions in the same method as each other, which it keeps in the transaction log. This process makes it possible to ensure that inputted data can change the database for each user. However, the number of people on the database at the same time may experience lags. For corporations with many dozens of people accessing the same database, transactions may be slow.

Smaller transactions not only improve speed in database processing, but they are also required to complete processing quickly. Refer to the discussion about commit and rollback transactions. If a transaction is short, it is likely to commit to the transaction and fulfill the request quickly. However, if a transaction becomes lengthy with multiple people accessing the information at the same time, the chances increase that the process will require a rollback. For lengthy transactions, therefore, it is suggested to limit access to fewer database ports.

Locking

When considering how many people have access to a database at the same time, it seems unlikely that a database would constantly morph to accommodate data inputted after every query in a SQL system. If data constantly changed as people adjusted data, it would be impossible to know if your data had been saved or not. SQL offers a way to create security in sending queries when multiple people access the database at the same time. The process is called locking.

Locking means just what it does in English. Once a transaction is completed, it is locked in the system, which means that someone else working on the same table cannot change the transaction when it is in progress or afterward. SQL creates a way to moderate how to input data by using locking to prevent data corruption.

Locking Granularity and Levels

Granularity takes into account the different levels of a process. The locking process has a significant number of levels which can range from large (the entire database) to small (simple blocks of data from a table). Locking at each level may be necessary at any point in time when creating an SQL database.

The largest locking level can lock the entire database. It is unwise to lock the database for more than a few minutes. If the database is extensive, other areas of a company will need access to data, and when transactions are inevitably performed, employees will need to process data. Locking the entire database may be necessary when scanning many tables or making major modifications. Locking the database does not mean that every section of the database will be used in a search or organizational change, but changing large numbers of tables may call for this.

The next step down in locking is on the table level. Since SQL is a relational database, a single table may be connected to multiple other tables, so locking one should also only be considered when few people have access to the database. Table-based transactions link transaction tables together, which means that each transaction may require extensive work. Though it is still possible for others to use the database during table locking, processes become slow.

Page-level locking involves pieces of data usually around the sizes of 4KB, 8KB, or 16KB, blocking out only parts of data tables. Pages involve only select sections of tables, so others using the database still have access to tables. Large amounts of data in tables is common, so involving page-level locking often means that the data runs in parallel.

Locking is also available at the row level, though it is usually avoided. When working in the organization of a database, defining rows seems like a small task, and locking off only specific rows often causes more damage than good. Though the information locked in these rows is not damaged, the processing time to complete transactions with row locking is substantially large. Though it is common to use page-level locking, row locking usually becomes too much of a hassle.

Locking on the data level is far more a theory than a practice. Though it is possible to lock only some data points, the lack of efficiency that comes with this method usually is enough to dissuade any programmer. Consider page and table locking when changing information in a database.

Shared and Exclusive Locks

Shared locks allow for data views from others using the database. Though shared locks do not allow updating, anyone on the database can view a shared lock for reference only. For instance, if a programmer updates an accounting record and puts a table in a lock, accountants still have the ability to pull reports from the database. This lock is especially effective in large companies that constantly require access to the database.

Exclusive locks, however, prevent employees from accessing the locked items at all, including running reports. Exclusive locks are most common on large scales. For example, a programmer may use an extensive lock to change all data associated with the costs of vehicles on the lot. Because the electricity bill has increased significantly, the dealership may require increasing the price of cars by 5%. An exclusive lock allows programmers to lock data viewing, whose reports may influence a customer's willingness to purchase a vehicle.

Deadlocks

Just as locking can lead to important changes in the database, it can also cause problems when multiple people place locks on the same data, which is known as a deadlock. Placing a lock on part of the database stops transaction processes, which could lead to a frozen database. Each transaction in process attempts to finish but also must wait for the other transaction to complete. Though a deadlock between two locks may occur, it is equally possible that many deadlocks prevent the database from continuing transactions. Unsophisticated SQL services could keep these in limbo forever.

Fortunately, SQL creates a way to rid itself of deadlocks. SQL effectively picks one of the two transactions and rolls it back, ending the process. The other transaction is then free to continue and completes the transaction. The failed transaction, however, will receive an error message, and the process will require the transaction to process again. If there are more than two – let us say in the lower double digits – SQL will choose a transaction at random to complete while the others receive a rollback and error message. All processes that failed require the process to run again.

Processes as simple as a SELECT query could be subject to a rollback. Processes that fail to complete are known as "losers," though they are more significant than the name implies. Though it may seem unfair that some simple queries result in errors, the alternative is far worse. Data corruption is caused by multiple queries simultaneously working and the system receiving incorrect information. The rollback failsafe, therefore, is an incredible benefit to the SQL system.

Isolation Levels

Databases must maintain a certain level of isolation when undergoing transactions. When processing transactions, the data must look the same for multiple people as they interact with the same data. Isolation occurs when someone is accessing and manipulating data and another is able to access that same data without returning different information.

Different levels of isolation affect the overall function of the database. When choosing an isolation level, consider the effect it may have on the rest of the database. Just like locking, isolation levels affect the way information is transmitted to people on the database. For example, if a dealership decides to halt all operations on a database when it is undergoing a vehicle sale, all access to that vehicle, customer, and process may be halted. On a large scale, isolating the sale process of a vehicle may prevent others from accessing sales information as well, even with sales unrelated to that customer or vehicle. Though it is possible to isolate transactions on a large scale, preventing operations in a large system and company may cause more damage than good. Though the process for that customer is safe, it prevents others from accessing vital data to complete their own transactions.

SERIALIZABLE Isolation

The SERIALIZABLE command is the highest level of isolation; it prevents processes from incurring any updates on a transaction when in use concurrently. Essentially, if data is being accessed and transactions are processed at the same time, neither user has the right to insert, edit, or delete information associated with the transaction. SERIALIZABLE isolation is required when expecting a database to read data the same way twice and return the same result (Colby & Wilton, 2005). Its command requires that concurrent processes will not change the end result of a query.

REPEATABLE READ Isolation

As the second strictest isolation, the REPEATABLE READ demands that all data in this isolation level must maintain its readable status. If queries update, insert, or delete data in a transaction while concurrently running with another user, the data must not change to accommodate those changes. Another row, however, may become available during a concurrent transaction. As a result, information may look as though it is added to the system, but the results will still read the same in a REPEATABLE READ.

READ COMMITTED Isolation

Only committed transactions are satisfied in the READ COMMITTED isolation. This is the third tier in isolation, and it provides a more relaxed view of a transaction. The defining credential in a REPEATABLE READ isolation is its ability to maintain a readable view of the transaction without any changes aside from the occasional phantom row that appears. READ COMMITTED isolation, however, requires a transaction be fully committed before it shows up in a current transaction. This isolation may be most common when dealing with smaller lines of data and locking. The system does not require complete dominance of the database, which means it may change at any time during the transaction.

READ UNCOMMITTED Isolation

This is the lowest tier in isolation. The only contingent for its existence is that any transaction may modify anyone's view of the transaction. The READ UNCOMMITTED isolation is subject to change at any time, which means that errors may occur regarding saved data. Any change to the transaction is noted, including inserts, updates, and deletion, making this isolation less popular for larger transactions. Uncommitted changes to a transaction may change the way a transaction behaves for someone working concurrently with another.

An RMDS generally defaults the READ UNCOMMITTED isolation to *read-only*, which means that any transactions under this isolation can only be seen, not modified. This prevents additional errors and change in transactions during a process. The *read-write* option for a READ UNCOMMITTED allows any user to change the data in a transaction at any time, regardless of concurrent transactions.

Summary

Transactions are a series of queries that work together to a logical conclusion. Data can be influenced through transactions, and they are marked complete only when they have received the COMMIT response. Transactions begin with the BEGIN TRANSACTION command and must continue until completion or receive the response ROLLBACK TRANSACTION. A saved transaction occurs when the command SAVE TRANSACTION saves individual steps in a transaction's progress. Without these saved transaction stopping points, if a process is interrupted, it must roll back to the beginning of the transaction and must be processed again.

Concurrent transactions can cause problems within a database if they are not properly formatted to include locking. Different levels of locking stop procedures from occurring, thereby saving information as it is processed. SERIALIZABLE isolation is the highest level of locking and requires that all transactions working concurrently within a system must not conclude until every view inside the table has concluded. the REPEATABLE READ isolation is next in line and allows for reading but saves information on the side to be saved later. The READ COMMITTED isolation allows others to see only committed transactions within its view, and the READ UNCOMMITTED allows for any views of the table to be seen, even those which have not completed as a transaction.

Chapter 9: Stored Procedures

As databases develop and become more adaptable, SQL offers a way to save information in the form of queries. Developing technology has made it possible for people outside the realm of programming to work with a database and make modifications that suit different situations. However, some technologies require the use of a programmer to change information within the system.

SQL has developed over the years to allow for stored procedures that work in the background of processes to keep the database running smoothly. Methods called *triggers* activate processes within the database and automatically fulfill transactions. For example, with the development of ACH, many programs now allow for the processing of payments while not at the office. These automatic transactions guide the database to deposit funds in the correct accounts and accurately report the results. SQL has developed enough to allow for stored procedures to affect a database behind the scenes.

Stored Procedure Basics

SQL was not originally designed to behave in a way that most programs do. The programming language was instead designed to work with basic queries and perform simple functions. It has developed over the years, however, to something more along the lines of what we see today in programming languages. It has developed over the years to have some of its own programmed basics.

As we have discussed before, conditional statements like IF, THEN, or ELSE allows the database to compare different statements and determine solutions to SQL queries.

WHILE or FOR are called *looping* queries that cause the database to run in a continued looping sequence until ordered to stop. Cursors, which are essentially locations in a query that define the separation of many rows to perform easier transaction functions, explain where these WHILE and FOR clauses stop the sequence. If the query is complex, it may result in the use of many cursors to define each query by layers.

SQL also stores functions by names and numeric operators, making it easy to access information regarding complex queries. SQL may save the name or number in future queries, making searching for information easier.

Creating a Stored Procedure

The CREATE PROCEDURE command creates a stored procedure, which can be updated as often as the programmer sees fit. All input parameters must then be assigned. Categories are defined, and commands are entered into the stored procedure. Column calculations are often defined through simple statements in SQL such as INSERT, UPDATE, or DELETE. These simple queries become the basis for the process of the stored procedure. As soon as a procedure is created, it can just as easily be dropped through the DROP PROCEDURE command.

Let us look at a basic example. Suppose the customers listed in a database require the same amount of work per entry, and a procedure is required to add customers more easily. All parameters for collecting data on the customer include the name, customer number, customer representative, and payments received.

```
/* Add customer procedure */

CREATE PROCEDURE Add_Customers

@c_name    varchar(15),         /* input customer
name */

@c_num     integer,                   /*        input
customer number */

@c_rep     varchar(15),         /* input sales rep
name */

@c_pay     integer,                   /* input pay
amount */
```

```
AS

BEGIN

        /* Insert new row from CUSTOMER table */

        INSERT INTO Customers (Cust_name, Cust_num,
Cust_rep, Cust_pay)

            values (@c_name, @c_num, @c_rep, @c_pay)

        /* Update row from SALESREP table */

        UPDATE SALESREP


        /* Commit transaction */

        COMMIT TRANS

END
```

Once completed, the EXECUTE command starts the procedure, storing the procedure for future use.

Cursors in Queries

As we discussed earlier, cursors moderate the procedures fulfilled in a query, and they are especially useful in the completion of a stored procedure. Just as closing a program to exit out of a file, a cursor effectively exits out of a query. Files and cursors use some of the same basic principles. They are defined by their ability to maintain a position in a software or program.

Cursors and files, however, are slightly different in the way they associate with their charges. For example, ending an application involves severing its tie to the file from which it is stored. That file then returns to its initial position in the program filing and can be accessed at the same point. Cursors, however, allow slightly more flexibility. Just as a mouse cursor follows the actions you make on your monitor, cursors in the SQL system keep tabs on where your query is in its process. Multiple cursors can also work in parallel to complete multiple actions in a database. The following cursors are those that control cursors in an SQL system.

DECLARE CURSOR

DECLARE CURSOR commands define sections of a query just as the SELECT statement defines locations in a table. When looking for a procedure in a database, the SELECT statement is used to find what query is associated with the cursor. The DECLARE CURSOR command requires the SELECT and FROM clauses to define where it is located. The DECLARE CURSOR command is simple and is only used to define the cursor. All systems that include cursors are effectively associated with this command and must become available through the command.

OPEN and CLOSE CURSOR

DECLARE CURSOR locates the cursors in an SQL system, and the OPEN CURSOR command demands that the query be completed. To access the query through the OPEN CURSOR command, the DECLARE CURSOR command must have located the query. Once a transaction is complete the RDMS automatically closes a query. The RDMS, however, must execute the CLOSE statement to finish the transaction.

FETCH CURSOR

In its most basic sense, the FETCH CURSOR finds statements within a query after it has been opened. The FETCH CURSOR command specifies which cursor and institutes the INTO clause, to determine the data received. The FETCH CURSOR command acts as a magnifying glass during a procedure, notifying the programmer of the results in every step of the query.

Cursor-Based Repetition

Cursors used in a stored procedure evaluate where a query lies in its transaction. The repetition of rows in a query requires cursors to specify its location. Once a stored procedure has begun, using the cursor-based repetition model to FETCH elements within the database requires a loop created by the

OPEN CURSOR command. The loop only completes when the CLOSE CURSOR command is applied.

Consider, for example, a dealership that sells two kinds of vehicles: motorhomes and houseboats. We wish to place the results into their respective accounts, but first, we have to wade through a large amount of data to define each vehicle. SQL must effectively create a system to insert data into each of these categories. Every row must be processed to find where all vehicles must be stored. SQL must come up with a method to search each of these vehicles on a loop until all vehicles are placed in the correct rows. With the cursor defined as O_VEHICLE, SQL must systematically work its way through the defined cursors to complete the process.

First, the DECLARE CURSOR command is required to define each section of the query. Next, the OPEN CURSOR allows for the procedure to commence. Since the query requires that the task must be repeated until all rows have been processed, the CLOSE CURSOR command is not immediately processed when the first row associated with the query completes. The FETCH command demands that each section of the table must be accessed, and it is continued in a loop until the CLOSE CURSOR command stops the query.

Summary

Stored procedures within a database make transactions and further queries within the database easier to accommodate. Stored procedures are created through the CREATE PROCEDURE command and are often used to save processes to make transactions with the database more automatic.

Cursors within databases can access queries and determine where they are in a process. The DECLARE CURSOR command shows where a cursor is located and allows the OPEN CURSOR and CLOSE CURSOR commands to process queries. SQL automatically closes queries unless otherwise specified. The FETCH CURSOR command shows steps in the process.

Cursor-based repetition gives the database queries that perform on loops and complete transactions in databases with quicker processing time.

Conclusion

SQL has been around for more than a few decades, but it continues to be one of the most impressive and most used databases in the industry. Not only is it easy to learn, but the subsequent weeks of practicing with the subject provide quick setups and easy software to use in running your company.

SQL is designed to make your life simpler when entering the business sector. Its easy commands to insert, update, and delete data creates an atmosphere of easy access to information throughout an entire company. Because it is designed in a relational database, the SQL database provides a background to easily organize and manipulate data.

Not only does SQL create tables in which to measure and see data, it also provides an organization to define data and express it through different commands. Any area of the database can be accessed through commands listed in this book. The commands listed are easy to follow and contain examples for your own benefit so you can easily navigate through the book when you have completed it. Keep in mind that the sections of this books are designed to help you easily navigate to sections in which you may not have understood the material well. This book should provide you the confidence to create your own database but also remain a guide for the rest of your SQL career.

This book should give you a basis for not only how to create a database, but how to order it so it becomes the most efficient and effective that it can be. There are many ways to organize the data listed in this book, but following commands that depend entirely on the welfare of the database, and best practices listed in this book will prepare your database for any errors of unusual activity you may experience when exploring SQL for yourself.

This book was designed to create a connection between SQL and everyday uses in a business. Creating, updating, and deleting tables is only the first step on the journey to creating a database that supports summaries, sorting, and data manipulation. Each query within the SQL system is designed to create fast processing and easy maintenance of the database that runs your company, hobby, or life.

Find a database online and begin practicing these activities. This beginner's guide to SQL will guide you through more than setting up a database, and the advanced levels within this book will allow you to create a database and manage it with ease.

Made in the USA
San Bernardino, CA
10 February 2020